strong

s Ramsey

NEBERGER Cloni Springs

Haggerty Sharpe

Sloan Thomas Pasour

Robinson Eldridge

Gullick Costner

Palmer Mauney

Rudisill

owe

d Wilkins Hambright RUTLEDGE

ick Patterson

Hovis Henry Black

er Rankin Cansler

Hoffman

History of Gaston County

To the people of Gaston County
and to all persons interested in her history,
this book is respectfully dedicated.

This portrait of Minnie Stowe Puett was painted in 1927 by T. Emile Dodamead. Mrs. Puett was then about fifty-six years old. The painting now hangs in the Belmont Public Library.
(Photo by Rick Haithcox Photography.)

History of Gaston County

by

Minnie Stowe Puett

Historian of Gaston County

Originally published April 1939

Reprint. Charlotte, North Carolina: Laney-Smith, Inc. 1998

LANEY-SMITH, INC.

Published by Laney-Smith, Inc.
1370 Briar Creek Road
Charlotte, North Carolina 28205

Telephone: 704 536-9832
Fax: 704 536-9834

Distribution by: Daniel Jonathan Stowe Foundation
Post Office Box 1046
Belmont, North Carolina 28012

Manufactured in the United States of America

First printing: 1939   Second printing: 1998

Library of Congress Cataloging in Publication Data

Puett, Minnie Stowe, 1871–1945
       History of Gaston County / by Minnie Stowe Puett.
            p.   cm.
       Originally published: Charlotte, N.C.: Observer Print. House,
       1939. Includes index.
       ISBN 0–9624488–8–5
       1. Gaston County (N.C.)— History.   2. Indians and
       Pioneers.   3. Battle of King's Mountain.   4. Beginning
       of Textile Industry, Gaston County. I. Title.
       F262.G2P8   1998
       975.6′773—dc21   96–29798
                                                          CIP

Credits:
       Design: Mary Charles Churchill-Nash
       Printing: Loftin & Company, Inc.

Cover photograph of the Backcountry Farm kitchen at the Schiele Museum in Gastonia, by Rick Haithcox Photography, Dallas, N.C.

ABOUT THE AUTHOR

Minnie Stowe Puett was born Minnie Leona Stowe on October 26, 1871. Her parents were Charles Theodore and Margaret Ann Sloan Stowe of the South Point community. Of Minnie's thirteen brothers and sisters, eight lived past childhood. In 1896, she married William Burgess Puett. William was born in Forsyth County, Georgia, and moved to Belmont in 1886 to work as the express agent and telegraph operator for Southern Railway. He filled that position until 1905 but also developed other interests.

Minnie attended the old Gaston College in Dallas, North Carolina. She showed promise as an artist and took a special art course at Sacred Heart Academy in Belmont. Under the tutelage of Professor F. P. Hall, she was instructed in a full Davidson College course. She later taught school in the Belmont area.

Mrs. Puett was very active in local and national issues. A keen interest in politics sparked her activism in the Democratic Party and the women's suffrage movement. Mrs. Puett was also a member of the United Daughters of the Confederacy and an organizer of the local Woman's Club. She was noted for her devotion to civic betterment, especially improvement in the textile communities.

Mrs. Puett played a vital role in the establishment of the first Belmont library, located in the former Woman's Club building on South Main Street. The current Belmont Public Library was dedicated in her honor in 1960.

Today, the Minnie Stowe Puett Papers are housed in the archives of the Gaston County Museum of Art and History. This collection evidences her wide range of interests, including travel, gardening, needlework, homemaking, and decorating. It also reveals her deep fascination with history — particularly the histories of Gaston County, North Carolina, the Civil War, and the South.

Mrs. Puett is buried at Greenwood Cemetery in Belmont.

PREFACE

When Minnie Stowe Puett, known in our family as "Aunt Min," wrote the introduction to this book, she dated the beginning of her work as "Several years ago," meaning several years prior to 1939. My research has established that her appointment as historian for Gaston County actually dates from 1927. Aunt Min lived within sight of our house back then, and my dad often commented that the light in her study had been on at five in the morning.

The objective of the Historical Commission of North Carolina was to see the history of each county written and preserved in some form. Research by George Stevenson of the North Carolina State Archives in 1996 established that these historians indeed took many different approaches, some publishing their work as a series of articles in local newspapers. Their timing reflected a similar diversity, in some instances extending even forty years after their appointments.

When I found myself with only two copies of the original book, I realized that it was time to reissue this invaluable history. We have been able to enrich this reprinted version with many photographs and illustrations.

In her history, Aunt Min gives sketches of some forty-five early families settling in the Gaston County area. For many of these, the exact age of the family head could only be approximated, and Aunt Min would record that "he lived to a ripe old age." But her scholarly research did establish birth and death dates for many pioneers. She specifically names seven who lived to be older than 90, with two reaching 101 and 104 years of age. Since they all died prior to 1939, at a time when life expectancy was shorter than it is today, their ages become even more impressive. Perhaps we have fountains of youth situated in our county. It is a happy possibility to accompany you through the pages of Aunt Min's reprinted history.

Daniel J. Stowe

Daniel J. Stowe

INTRODUCTION

SEVERAL years ago, the Historical Commission of North Carolina started a movement to have the history of the State preserved, beginning with the county as a unit. The plan was to appoint a historian for each county. These historians were to preserve the data in any way that seemed advisable. A history for each county seemed the only adequate way.

The historians were to be appointed by the County Board of Education of the several counties and were to be approved by the Secretary of the North Carolina Historical Commission, who at that time was Dr. A. R. Newsome. He is now head of the History Department of the University of North Carolina.

The position for Gaston County was offered to and accepted by the author of this book. It was readily realized that the task would be long and hard. At that time almost nothing had been done to preserve the county's history. There had been bits of history written and placed here and there in other histories, but Gaston had no book of her own. Much of the county's noblest history had been made by pioneers and other colonists while Gaston bore another name, but it was made by her own people who lived on her own soil and Gaston has a right to claim it as her own.

Many Gaston County people have helped to make this book possible. Many facts almost forgotten and many gleanings from the past were called forth to become a part of this book. In the crucial days of research, the late Mrs. G. A. Sparrow and Miss Corinne Puett were tireless in their efforts to help. To these and to all others who rendered aid in any way, grateful acknowledgment is extended.

MINNIE STOWE PUETT

Belmont, North Carolina
April, 1939

CONTENTS

ILLUSTRATIONS

Aerial view of South Point area, showing confluence of the South Fork and Catawba rivers. (Photo by Rick Haithcox Photography.)

CHAPTER I

GASTON COUNTY: GEOGRAPHICAL FEATURES,
CHARACTER OF SOIL, FLORA, AND FAUNA

The territory now known as Gaston County was making history long before it was called Gaston or had well-defined boundaries. It is a small county located in the Piedmont section of the State of North Carolina. In area it is about 363 square miles. Its surface is rolling and hilly. The Catawba River forms its eastern boundary and separates it from Mecklenburg County. The principal stream dividing its area is the South Fork of the Catawba, a beautiful river, formed by the union of two creeks, Jacob's Fork and Henry Creek, springing from the foothills of the Blue Ridge in Burke County. It severs the dividing line between Lincoln and Gaston about centrally, and flows in a southeasterly direction the entire length of the county, joining the Catawba River near the South Carolina line.

Several large creeks flow across parts of it, Crowder's, Catawba, Big and Little Long Creeks, Stanley, and Dutchman's. Additional named creeks are Taylor's, Holland, Duhart, Fite's, South Prong, Beaver Dam, and perhaps others. Streams, many of them not named, just spoken of as the branch on a certain farm, come forth, like throbbing arteries, from clear, cold springs at the foot of the hills, and joining the larger streams form a network which drains the county admirably.

Gaston County is rich in a life-giving climate, brilliant skies, and fertile lands and steeps that could be pastured and made profitable for the raising of cattle, pigs, and sheep.

CHARACTER OF SOIL

Gaston County is on the Piedmont plateau which lies at the eastern foot of the Blue Ridge. It is really an ancient lowland worn almost to a plain. It expands in Virginia and the Carolinas to a width of about one hundred miles, and on it most of the larger towns are situated. The hills are usually low and gentle, but occasionally there rises a rugged eminence which is a landmark for the countryside. Several such elevations stand out prominently, namely: Crowder's Mountain, Spencer Mountain, Pasour's, Whetstone at Bessemer City, and Little Mountain in the Robinson section of Union. The hills and occasional peaks relieve the landscape from the monotony of the level plains.

In a few localities, noticeably on the hilltops near the Catawba River, there are many round, polished stones showing the action of running water and proving that at some period of the earth's history the hilltops were the beds of streams. But the most important rocks are the granites, the gneisses which are composed of quartz, feldspar, and mica, and another variety designated as schists. Granite is to be seen around Gastonia, Union Church, Dallas, High Shoals, northeast of McAdenville, and between Dallas and Bessemer City. Around Cherryville, to the west of Mountain Island, a very rough grained granite is found. The disintegration of the granites has formed the coarse sandy loams. There are smaller areas where other granites and gneisses have formed the finer sandy loams. To the east of Pasour's Mountain and Bessemer City, there is a fine grained soapstone which has changed, to some extent, the sandy loam found there.

On the mountain peaks quartzite is the principal rock. It is a hard, weather resisting stone and is probably the solution of the existence of the lone peaks which have stood as sentinels as the generations of Red Men and white have come and gone.

Throughout the various formations, veins of quartz are to be found and fragments of this rock persist in the soil.

The county is in the Carolina gold belt which crosses the state diagonally, entering South Carolina through York County.

While numerous soils are found, yet two of the finest of the great Piedmont section comprise more than half of the area of the county. These are clay and sandy loams. The clay loams cover about twenty-eight percent of the county. This soil is usually called red land. Sometimes it is sandy and pliable; sometimes tough, stiff red clay. The other type, or sandy loam, occurs in rolling areas extending north and south through the central part of the county. These soils are all adapted to the growth of cotton, corn, hay, fruits, vegetables, and grain crops.

FLORA

The flora of the county is beautiful and varied. There are areas still classified as forest lands. Much of this, however, has had the greater part of all saleable timber cut from it; but there are yet enough trees left that in the words of John Muir: "We may learn how they live and behave in pure wildness, rejoicing in the storm, putting forth their new leaves and flowers when all the streams are in flood and the birds singing, and sending away their seeds in the summer when all the landscape is glowing in deep, calm enthusiasm—for this you must love them and live with them, as free from selfishness, care and time as the trees themselves."

While some varieties, as the chestnut, the buckeye, and the cucumber or magnolia, have about disappeared, many, well worth knowing, still remain. The short leaf pine, also known as the Rosemary pine, the yellow pine, and the old field pine are widely distributed, but the great type of American forest, the deciduous, is more prevalent. Often the pine and cedar are mixed with it in a beautiful blending of color. The deciduous trees have broad leaves which they cast off each winter. Early frosts coming suddenly bring a blaze of glory and a brilliance of color not surpassed in any other part of the world. There is a delicate blending of color and harmony which is of the greatest charm, and its contrast with the green of summer or the bare branches of winter adds a variety which is lacking in all other kinds of forest.

Deciduous trees grow best in well-balanced regions where the seasons are not unduly long and there is an approaching of equality in summer and winter, and where neither is subject to long drouths. The short leaf pine, oak, walnut, and poplar are our most valuable timber trees. Hickory is a fine wood for baskets and chairs. As a fuel, it makes beds of glowing coals. The white-winged elm, the maple, and the linden are used largely for shade where the oak does not grow naturally. The beech is one of the most beautiful of all trees either in summer or winter. The glowing leaves of the gum distinguish it in the autumn. Along the streams we have the sycamore, a favorite of the children because in the days when toys were scarce they had good times playing with its balls.

Interspersed with the deciduous trees are the smaller trees and shrubs, the aromatic sassafras, the red maple, and the red bud, sometimes called the Judas tree from its relative in the Orient on one of which Judas is supposed to have hanged himself. These latter are the first to bring color to the spring-time woods. The honey locust sometimes grows in the forest, but more often in fence corners and waste places beside roads; and not uncommonly it marks the home site of some Gaston County pioneer. The dogwood with its wealth of snow-white blossoms in spring, followed by red berries in winter, occupies a place of honor among our shrubs.

Among the evergreens the white cedar, sometimes called the Carolina Juniper, likes open spaces, such as old fields, and lends great beauty to the landscape because of its upright, conical growth. On the hillsides the dark red of the sweet shrub and the pink of the wild honeysuckle call forth exclamations of delight. Along old fence rows the wild cherry, the black haw, and the chinaberry mingle with the smooth sumac, a showy plant bearing clusters of red berries and bright leaves. The trumpet creeper, with its trumpet-shaped scarlet flowers, growing luxuriantly along branches and creeks, covering rocks or stumps, and perchance climbing the modern telephone pole, is a vision of rare beauty.

Great patches of oxeye daisies make glad the June days, while asters and goldenrod brighten the September fields. On warm days in early spring, children of many generations have sought the forest glades to find the very first of the wild flowers, or anemones, the bloodroot, the hepatica, and many others—the first messengers of spring. Many of the indigenous plants had Indian names, as *pipsissewa* for Prince's pine, and were used by the Indians for medicines and dyes. Their identification and use were learned by the early settlers from the Indians and handed down from generation to generation, and even to this day their virtues are recognized and they are compounded in many ways.

While some of the more persistent are left, many of the wild flowers, which once made our hills and dales glow with color and were entwined in garlands to deck the beauty of dusky Indian maidens, have given way to the inroads of commercial progress; but others of these blossoming children are still carrying on a persistent warfare on behalf of their right to exist. Some are natives; others came as stowaways in the boats that brought the pioneers. Among the few valued possessions, carefully guarded and cherished by our grandmothers, were often packages of seeds or plants, coming with their owners who were seeking a chance to find a new home and to lay the foundation of another colony of their kind.

In addition to the trees and flowers, grasses prevail over the entire county except in the forests. The story of the grasses began even before the age of man. They were necessary for the maintenance of animal life and soon became the natural overseers of the ground. Were it not for them the soil would be as shifting as the sands, riding on the raindrops as they go on their journeys to the sea. The grasses hold the land in place and compel it to do its duty as becomes a faithful servant of man.

Our food grasses are wheat, corn, oats, barley, and rye. The smaller, or pigmy, grasses have long furnished pasturage for domestic animals. We need the grasses, and some of them, especially the food grasses, need us. Others have known nothing but to fight for themselves. Traveling along the roads they have scattered their seeds until they have gained a foothold which insures for them a permanent home. Not only have they established themselves; but, since it was necessary for the first settlers to have grazing ground for their cattle, the grasses which were found in great treeless areas of what is now Gaston County, had much to do with the locations of the homes of pioneers.

FAUNA

The fauna added interest and helped mightily in supplying food for both Indian and white man. The Catawba and South Fork Rivers teemed with catfish, perch, suckers, and red-horse, the latter delightful for food but now rarely seen. The woods were alive with birds of beautiful plumage. Many squirrels chattered in the tree tops and were easy game for the hunter. Wild turkeys abounded. At certain seasons of the year migrating birds, such as geese and ducks, were plentiful along the streams.

Rabbits hid in many a coppice, and covies of quail, which hunters never dreamed of shooting but took with nets, were found wherever food was plentiful. "Coon and possum" hunting was great sport. Wildcats were numerous, deer stalked the forests, and occasionally a bear was seen.

Such was the flora and the fauna when the colonization of the county began.

CHAPTER II

THE CATAWBA INDIANS

Gaston County is part of the ancestral grounds of the once powerful Catawba Indians. They had their homes on the banks of the river bearing their name, but it is known by the numbers of arrows and other implements plowed up in the fields that their hunting grounds covered most of the county and other territory. They presented a wonderful example of faithfulness and devotion to the American people. Indeed, many times did the woods of Carolina ring with their war whoops as they went forth to battle with the Cherokees and other enemies of the early settlers. Later, many of them fought during the war of the Revolution to help their white neighbors gain their independence, and more than once they marched under the Colonial flag against their own race.

Interesting would their records be; but, alas, the story of only a few of their deeds has been preserved, and the only reminders that the present inhabitants of the county have of their former existence are their names and graves containing many relics, such as beads, arrows, hatchets, tomahawks, and pottery, which are occasionally uncovered by the plow or a great freshet.

With the coming of the white man the savage glory of the Indian began to pass away, the primeval forests were laid low, the rude log cabins of the whites replaced the tepees of the Red Men, and the Indians were gradually driven from the haunts they loved. Their name was given to the river by which their council fires were lighted and where their peace pipes were smoked, and where baskets were woven and pottery moulded by their women. May the name, at least, be unchanged and left to perpetuate a nation's memory and to remind successive generations of other peoples that here the Catawba Indians lived and loved and died, and from here went to join their forefathers in the happy hunting grounds of the Great Spirit.

The Indians, as is well known, are a race of traditions, being entirely destitute of written records; therefore, it is not strange that the origin of the Catawbas is not known with absolute certainty.

One of the alleged traditions which does not agree in any of the main points with the known facts of history is: "The Catawbas came here from the north in 1660 as refugees from the French and their Indian allies. On arrival at the Catawba River their progress was disputed by the Cherokees, who claimed original ownership of the country. A terrible battle ensued. At nightfall eleven hundred Cherokees and a thousand Catawbas lay dead on the field. The battle was a draw; a truce was declared, the Catawbas taking the Catawba River valley and the Cherokees that of the Broad River and beyond. The Broad River was henceforth called Eswau Huppeday (line river) by the Catawbas." The above may have referred to some local incident, but hardly to a tribal movement.

The Catawbas were classed as a distinct stock until Gatschet in 1881 pronounced them Siouan because he found in their language Siouan correspondences. It has been claimed that the home of the Sioux was at one time in the upper Ohio valley from which place one branch migrated to the east, another to the west. Later investigations have proved, by linguistic forms and traditional evidence, that several other tribes of the same region as the Catawbas were also of Siouan stock. All investigations point to this eastern region as the original home of the Sioux and consequently of the Catawbas, whose tribe was probably the most important of the eastern Siouan tribes.

The source of the name is uncertain. Gatschet supposed it came from Choctaw Katapau which means divided, because of their separation or division from the Sioux.

While they were mentioned in 1579 by Vandera in his narrative of Pardo's expedition and again in 1670 by Lederer, nothing was really known of them until Lawson, the surveyor and historian, passed through their territory in 1701. He spoke of them as a powerful nation and stated that their villages were very thick. From all accounts they were the most important tribe in the Carolinas with the exception of the Cherokees. Virginia traders were already among them at the time of Lawson's visit. Adair, seventy-five years later, said that one of the ancient cleared fields of the tribe extended seven miles. In 1728 they still had six villages, all on the Catawba River. (Handbook of American Indians). During the early part of the 18th century there was perhaps no more powerful tribe of Indians on the American continent, from the standpoint of warrior strength, than the Catawba.

About 1720 there lived among them a mighty chief, the story of whose bravery has been dug up out of the records and traditions of the past. His name was Sapona. He roamed the forest with the braves in search of the deer, the bear, and the fox. He knew where the red-horse, the catfish, and the trout were most plentiful in the tawny waters of the Catawba. It was his directing voice that could be heard above the others around the council fires; his advice that was wisest, safest, best. Sapona's frame was powerful. His eye was as the piercing eye of the eagle. During this period the known history of the tribe is chiefly a record of petty warfare with the Iroquois and other northern tribes. The name Sapona struck terror to the hearts of these, the enemies of the Catawbas, from time immemorial. Because he was once captured by the Senecas and, after making his escape, killed five of their number as they lay in their camp, the warriors thought his a charmed life and called him Astugah, the Great Wizard.

Sapona had many of the qualities most admired by Indians. The ability to kill was one test of greatness. More than 200 scalps dangled from his tepee during his lifetime. In taking them he had many narrow escapes from death, but his aim was sure and his execution swift. He had wisdom in council and power in war. Great was Sapona of the Catawbas.

About the time of Sapona, the strength and power of the tribe began to decline. Their loss was ceaseless from the attacks of their enemies. In 1738 smallpox worked great destruction among them. In 1759 it appeared again, this time destroying nearly half the tribe, due to the virulent type of the disease and their ignorance of the proper treatment. As soon as attacked, they exposed their bodies to a very high temperature in a kind of oven and then jumped into the waters of the river. Scaife said, "For a long time the woods were offensive with their dead bodies, which became the prey of dogs, wolves, and vultures."

In a sketch of Thomas Spratt, the first white man, so far as known, to live among the Catawbas, an interesting account of the Indians is given. The sketch was written by a grandson, also named Thomas Spratt. It was loaned by John D. McLean and copied by Melva and Virginia Leeper. Spratt told of his father's having been bitten by a rattlesnake when he was a boy, and that "Old New River," the Indian chief, sucked the wound and got mighty sick.

The elder Spratt acted as governor among the Indians and had many dealings with New River, who derived his name from a celebrated victory he gained over the Shawnees on New River in Virginia. On one occasion Spratt loaned New River a horse. The chief got drunk and when he mounted did not notice that one of the stirrups was under the saddle. He rode all the way home with it in that position, badly bruising and cutting the horse's back. Spratt was quite angry and dealt severely with New River.

Spratt reared a young Indian who was left an orphan by smallpox. He named him Peter Harris, the first Catawba ever to bear an English name. His descendants are among the few full bloods now living on the Catawba Reservation in York County, South Carolina. Harris served in the Revolutionary War, being in several engagements. After the war he and two other Indians were taken by white men to England and Ireland. They were likely the first Catawbas to glimpse any part of the old world. When the strength of this old soldier was declining and he saw his race almost extinguished, he made for his people the following eloquent appeal which deserves to be preserved: "I am one of the lingering survivors of an almost extinguished race. Our graves will soon be our habitations. I am one of the few stalks that still remain in the field after the tempest of the Revolution. I fought the British for your sake. The British have disappeared, nor have I gained by their defeat. I pursued the deer for a subsistence; the deer are disappearing and I must starve. God ordained me for the forest, and my ambition is for the shade. But the strength of my arm decays, and my feet fail me in the chase. The hand which fought the British for your liberties is now open for your relief. In my youth I bled in battle that you might be independent. Let not my heart in my old age bleed for want of your commiseration."

On one occasion the Indians, in order to induce Spratt to live among them, promised him their protection and all the land he wanted. According to the records of the survey about 4700 acres were given, most of which he sold or gave away.

While Spratt never lived in what is now Gaston County, his association with the Catawbas, who dwelt on both sides of the river and whose territory covered a large part of what was Anson County from 1749 to 1762, touched them all vitally since they were under the same chiefs and there were no territorial divisions as now prevail.

One of the most noted chiefs of the Catawbas was King Haiglar. Though a monarch of a savage tribe, there were elements of justice and right in his character which must be admired by those who live in a higher condition of life. The following story well illustrates one of his distinctive qualities: "Once a Frenchman, who was a great fiddler, was traveling through the country. The Indians were charmed and looked in wonder at the box from which the mysterious music came. One of them was so infatuated that he lay in ambush and murdered the poor musician to get possession of the fiddle. The news spread and the whites appealed to Spratt for protection. He went to King Haiglar and laid the case before him. The King promised that justice should be done and blew a piercing blast on his hunting horn. Soon the Indians began collecting from every quarter, while the King stood alert with his rifle resting in the hollow of his arm. At length the guilty Indian appeared, carrying a deer upon his back. Without a word of warning King Haiglar raised his rifle and shot him through the heart." Thus was the musician's death avenged. This is the only known record of a white man's ever having been murdered by a Catawba.

Scaife in his "History and Conditions of the Catawba Indians" stated that "another incident in Haiglar's life is the fact that he was probably the first person to present a temperance petition in the Carolinas." The following petition to Chief Justice Henley, dated May, 1756, was found in the State Archives of North Carolina: "I desire a stop may be put to the selling of strong liquors by the white people to my people. If the white people make strong drink, let them sell it to one another or drink it in their own families. This will avoid a great deal of mischief, which will happen otherwise from my people getting drunk and quarreling with the white people."

During one of the frequent raids of the Shawnees on the white settlers near the Catawba River, King Haiglar was shot and scalped, in the year 1762, by seven Shawnee Indians. He was greatly beloved and venerated by his people, and no man could have been more sincerely mourned.

From the time of the death of King Haiglar, the Catawbas ceased to be of importance except in conjunction with the whites. They had but one more king after Haiglar. When the Americans declared independence and threw monarchy overboard, the

Indians followed their example. The king after Haiglar was named Soe or Froe. After a few years' reign he was killed in a war with the Cherokees, and New River, previously mentioned, succeeded him under the title of general.

About the year 1764, a treaty between the Catawba Indians and the province of South Carolina was made and signed at Augusta, Georgia. This was probably the first treaty that the Catawbas made with the white people regarding their lands, and by the terms of it 144,000 acres on the Catawba River were confirmed to the tribe . . . The North and South Carolina boundary line between York and Gaston Counties was not established until 1772 . . .

In a campaign against the hostile Cherokees, whom the British incited to commence a series of brutal massacres upon the frontiers of Carolina, a large number of Catawbas marched against them and several were killed.

After the battle of Ramseur's Mill, thirty-five Indian warriors under their chief, New River, joined Major Davie near the South Carolina line where he had been ordered by General Rutherford to protect this exposed frontier from invasion by the British and Tories.

Near the close of the Revolution the entire tribe, or at least their women and children, were compelled by the British to remove to Virginia as a place of greater safety, by which move they lost their stock and everything they could not take with them. They remained about eighteen months, during which time many of their warriors were in active service in the American army. They were always loyal and made excellent guides, scouts, and runners. No Catawba was ever known to be a Tory.

Their attitude toward the whites was peaceful and friendly. Their worst faults were indolence and improvidence. There is now only a fast diminishing remnant of Catawbas left. They live on the reservation in York County, South Carolina. Tribal government has passed away. So-called chiefs are still elected, but they are without power. The selection is a very simple matter. Someone is nominated and the vote is taken by the raising of right hands. The same party is often re-elected. They are wards of the state and cannot vote or hold land as individuals. The lands are non-taxable and may be leased but not sold. They have never given the government any trouble and in turn have been almost forgotten by it. All the remnant of the tribe, with the exception of about a dozen, are Mormons. They are kindly, hospitable, and intelligent. When visited lately by the writer, they were found to have a good school with a teacher interested in their welfare. The children's love of flowers was evidenced by little clusters on their desks. One little girl made an offering to the visitors of wild buttercups, rooster fights, and sour grass.

The women still make pottery by hand. One woman, Sallie Gordon, a full blood and half sister of the present Chief Blue, showed us how it is done. After formation, the pieces are scraped with a shell and polished with a stone handed down from one generation to another. Sallie said the one she used was six hundred years old. She knows English, but, at request, talked in the musical Catawba tongue which will soon be forever stilled.

Descendants of Peter Harris are still among them. One of them, David Adam Harris, while very poor, is intelligent and quite interesting. He has a son who went to France as a soldier during the World War.

A little agriculture is carried on among them, but the main industry is the old art of pottery making by the women. It is sold to visitors and in stores, and is sometimes carried to distant towns and sold from house to house.

The great flood of the Catawba, in 1916, uncovered in the bend of the river on the A. M. Henderson place, skeletons, beads, pottery, arrows and spearheads, one metal pot, and the charred remains of a furnace where pottery was baked. Some of the beads were most interesting, being made of the teeth of animals; others, a dark brown, were formed of clay. Some were turquoise blue, a few glass beads were dark blue, some small beads were black and sleek, and others were of stone. Children living in the vicinity gathered great quantities of them and strung them into beautiful necklaces. Most glass beads that the Indians had were made in England and were obtained from traders who came among them as early, if not earlier, than 1700. The first glass beads of American make were manufactured near Jamestown, Virginia. Many relics were found also, after the 1916 freshet, at Rock Island in the Point section. There is an Indian burying ground just back of the former home, in the Point, of the late John D. Hall. The children of the Hall family amused themselves gathering beads when it was necessary for them to carry water to men plowing near the ancient cemetery. In the lower part of the county, near the home of Mrs. Mollie Abee, there has been located, in an open field, a place where arrows were made in great quantities. This is indicated by the number found. On a near-by hillside is the quarry from which the stone was taken.

Some of the traditions of the Indians have been handed down and will be remembered. Future generations will know of their loyalty to the whites, and how they frequently went to war with the Cherokees and other tribes to protect their white neighbors; but when questioned concerning the mounds in their burying places, the look on their faces expresses the reply of Hiawatha:

> "On the grave-posts of our fathers
> Are no signs, no figures painted,
> Who are in those graves we know not,
> Only know they are our fathers."

Numbers of them sleep near the waters of the river they loved so well—beyond is the land of enchantment where many of their youthful dreams were born.

Congress has recently made some investigations and will surely see to it that the remaining Catawbas are well taken care of. They ask but little—

the right to exist and that their young men may
make a living by the sweat of their brows, and that
the older ones may go into the sunset and the presence of the Great Spirit with minds and hearts at
peace.

When the golden Indian summer comes, a legend
tells us that we may see the spirits of the Red Men
come back to play, and that the hazy, misty look
away off yonder across the fields are Indian spirits
marching along and dancing in the sunlight, and
that those objects like shocks of corn are really
Indian tepees. The smoky smell in the air is their
campfires smoldering and their pipes agoing. Some
say it's leaves burning, but those who know say it's
campfires and that the Indians dance around when
the moon is hanging low over the hill and the harvest
fields are swimming in its light. When the leaves
turn red in the fall, it is just another sign that the
Indian spirits are rustling, creeping, and whispering
among them. Every once in a while a leaf gives way
under some fat, old Indian ghost and comes splash-
ing down to the ground. The red color is the war
paint rubbing off the ghost. Pretty soon the Indians
go marching away, but next year they will come
trooping back. The sky will again be hazy with
them and their campfires will be burning.

The records show that the Scotch-Irish were a thrifty people of whom it is said that "they keep the Sabbath and everything else they get their hands on."

The term Scotch-Irish does not signify a mixed race. They are as pure Scotch as those of their countrymen who came to North Carolina directly from Scotland. . . . Neither the Irish nor the Scotch would ever have hyphenated the name.

CHAPTER III

COLONIZATION OF THE COUNTY

THE SCOTCH-IRISH

To understand the present it is necessary to know the past. To understand the history of any country or section of country one must know its hills and vales, its climate and its products, and the relation it bears to other parts of the country and to the world. His knowledge, however, must go beyond this. He must know how to estimate properly the influence of man's various environments in altering his energy and capacity and moulding his character in one direction or another. He must know the paths by which the inhabitants reached their present homes and the circumstances which induced their adventuring. The growth and development of Gaston County have been more profoundly influenced by the inheritances of its people from other lands than by its own physical aspects.

History, viewed broadly, is a record of man's migrations from one environment to another. Ever since Columbus pointed the way by sailing over tractless seas and the Elizabethan sea dogs charted other channels of navigation, America has been the last great goal of these migrations.

It may be said that three streams of migration have determined our history. The first, so remote as to be beyond the memory of man, is supposed to have brought the Indians from Asia. They possessed the land and held it unmolested, in undisputed possession, until the second and by far the most important stream rolled at flood tide from Europe and wrested from the Indians the land regarded as their own. The third stream flowed from Africa. It was charted by Europeans and brought the Negro race to our shores.

The Scotch-Irish and the Germans were the main sources of the European stream which spread over the Piedmont North Carolina and brought the pioneers to Gaston County. The English came later.

During the four decades from 1735 to the beginning of the Revolutionary War, two branches of the European stream, flowing principally from the settlements in Pennsylvania, spread far and wide over the fertile plains and valleys of central North Carolina. They were composed, for the most part, of emigrants of German and Scotch-Irish descent. The Scotch-Irish, somewhat in advance of the Germans, reached Gaston County in considerable numbers about 1750.

The term Scotch-Irish does not signify a mixed race. They are as pure Scotch as those of their countrymen who came to North Carolina directly from Scotland. They are in reality Scotch who once resided in Ireland. We shall now consider them as a people and their migrations and causes which, in the providence of God, finally placed them in Gaston County.

The Scotch-Irish were lowland Scotch transplanted to northern Ireland. The name Scotch-Irish

is a geographical and not a racial term. Between them
and the native Irish there was never a feeling of
friendship. The Irish despised the Scotch as usurp-
ers and conquerors; the Scotch, proud of their country and their race, treated the Irish with scorn and
contempt. This, together with their religious differences, fixed a gulf between the two peoples so wide
that rarely did they intermarry. This accounts for
the fact that, though they lived side by side for
generations, they were separated by a great chasm
of racial, social, political, and religious differences
which was never bridged. Each was determined that
his blood was not to be contaminated by mixture
with the other. Neither the Irish nor the Scotch
would ever have hyphenated the name. This was
done in America by the Pennsylvania Quakers, who
cared not for their antagonisms. The natives of
Ireland were almost entirely Roman Catholic, and
the descendants of the Scotch were Irish Presbyterians. Why then were these Protestants in the very
stronghold of Catholicism; why were they there and
from what place did they come? Ireland was a conquered country, but its people were insubordinate
and had long given England no end of trouble. In
the sixteenth and seventeenth centuries there seemed
no solution to their problems. Conditions were
especially bad in the ten districts of Ulster and
reached their height during the reign of Queen
Elizabeth. Each of these districts was presided over
by a military commander and a bishop of the
Church of England, who so aggravated the people

that, led by their chiefs, they were continuously breaking out in rebellion. After each reverse the British government confiscated the lands of the conquered, until finally most of the six large counties of Ulster passed into the hands of the British.

After the death of Elizabeth, James VI of Scotland ascended the throne of England as James I. Soon after he became king he was faced by the arduous task of solving the difficulties of Ulster, where the English government was scarcely recognized. He planned to take possession of that great country and to replace the Irish Catholics with Scotch Protestants.

He naturally turned for his settlers to the Scottish lowlands which are separated from the north of Ireland by the North Channel, only about twenty miles wide. The lands of Ulster were surveyed, the people began to arrive, and by 1619 there were as many as thirty or forty thousand lowland Scotch settled in Ulster. The venture was a success. The wilds of Tyrone began to teem with life. Flax was raised, and linen and woolen goods were produced not only for themselves but also for exportation to England. This was the first migration of the lowland Scotch, and thus was laid the foundation of an economic prosperity which was one of the sources of their second migration. The other was their religious beliefs giving offense to the bishops and clergy of the established Church of England.

During the next hundred years the linen and woolen industries grew and developed. Belfast, Londonderry, and other manufacturing cities arose out of the swamps of Ulster. Business was not in a thriving condition in England at the close of the seventeenth century, and to the woolen trade of Ireland was attributed the cause. The British Parliament petitioned the King for protection. He in turn commanded the Irish Parliament to pass an act forbidding the exportation of woolen goods from that country. Later, a second act forbade the exportation of such goods to any country except England. The English were then able to fix their own prices for the Irish products. Under the reign of Queen Anne, who succeeded James I, the High Church party of England, led by the bishops, ruled the Irish Parliament and passed a series of laws forbidding the Roman Catholic religion and greatly restricting that of the Presbyterians. A law known as the Test Act was passed which required all government officials to take communion according to the forms of the Church of England. Since all such places were held by Protestants, they were driven from their offices. This was followed by fines and imprisonment. Doors of Presbyterian churches were nailed up and an effort was made to have marriages which had been performed by Presbyterian ministers declared illegal and void.

Their industries crippled and their religious liberties interfered with, the Scotch-Irish began looking to America for relief, and for the fifty years before the beginning of the American Revolution they left Ireland in crowds, never to go back again.

Their migration from Ulster began about 1718. Many left when the woolen trade was destroyed;

others were driven away by the Test Act. Annual
shiploads left Belfast and Londonderry until the
spell of tyranny was broken in 1782.

The deeds of the Gaston County Scotch-Irish at
King's Mountain and other places are well known,
but are rarely connected with the resentment against
the English which continued to burn, after they
reached their new homes, because of their persecu-
tions in Ulster.

Most of them landed at Philadelphia, though
some came by way of Charleston and followed the
streams to the hill country of the Carolinas. Many
of them who landed at Philadelphia bought lands
in Pennsylvania and settled there; others moved
southward into the western part of Virginia and
North Carolina. Several reasons are given for this
third migration of the Scotch-Irish. One was the
high prices of land in Pennsylvania due to the landing of many settlers there who came not only from
Ireland, but also from Holland, Great Britain, and
Germany. Another reason was that during the years
from 1734 to 1765, the Governors of North Carolina, Gabriel Johnston from Scotland, and Matthew
Rowan and Arthur Dobbs from Ulster, were active
in their efforts to induce Scotch and Scotch-Irish
immigrants to settle in North Carolina. Through
these three men and their friends, North Carolina
was better known in southern Scotland and northern Ireland than in any other part of the old world.
Still another reason given was harsh treatment by
the Pennsylvania Quakers. When the invitation of
William Penn, inviting persecuted Christians from

all lands to his province, reached the Scotch-Irish in Ulster, many of them, already on the lookout for new homes, decided to come to Philadelphia.

The Quakers did not regard the newcomers as highly as had been hoped. They called them a pernicious and pugnacious people and gave them the name of Scotch-Irish. One old Ulster minister called it an ill-mannered name. Ill-mannered or not, it has lived to outgrow its reproach. The common anxiety was that if they continued to come they would make themselves proprietors of the province. The Quakers feared the Scotch-Irish as the Puritans had once feared the Quakers, and pushed them back to the frontier where they were compelled to bear the brunt of the Indian wars and to defend not only themselves but every hearthstone in the colony. Their lives were one perpetual struggle to maintain their homes from the Indians. So under the guiding hand of Providence many of them left Pennsylvania to scatter over North Carolina, which place was favorably situated for the building of a great commonwealth. Thus the three migrations of the Scotch-Irish, from lowland Scotland to Ireland, from Ireland to Philadelphia, and from Philadelphia to North Carolina, finally placed them in Gaston County. The route they took from Pennsylvania to reach their future homes in North Carolina is plainly shown on the maps of that day. Colonel William L. Saunders, in his prefatory notes in Colonial Records of North Carolina, Vol. V., p. XXI, has the following to say with regard to the road: "On Jeffrey's map, a copy of which is in the

Congressional Library at Washington, there is plainly laid down a road called 'the Great Road from the Yadkin River through Virginia, distant 435 miles.' It ran from Philadelphia through Lancaster and York Counties, Pennsylvania, to Winchester, Virginia, thence up the Shenandoah valley, thence southward crossing the Dan River." Colonel Saunders, continuing, said: "Remembering the route Gen. Lee took when he went into Pennsylvania, in that memorable Gettysburg campaign, it will be seen that very many of the North Carolina boys, both of German and Scotch-Irish descent, in following their great leader, visited the homes of their ancestors and went hither by the very route by which they had come away."

The first of the Scotch-Irish came to the state in 1735 and went to the Moravian settlements. About 1750 another tide of Scotch-Irish flowed into the state going westward into what is now Mecklenburg, Lincoln, and Gaston Counties. In 1762 Mecklenburg, of which Gaston was then a part, became the center of the Scotch-Irish settlements. The rapidity with which the settlers came caused the erection of six new counties within sixteen years. The county farthest to the west extended to the mountains and beyond. When a new county was formed from one already existing, it was known that the white population had moved farther west.

The Scotch-Irish were industrious, independent, self-reliant, and deeply religious. They remembered that their ancestors had signed the Scottish covenant with their own blood and they were willing that their blood in turn should flow in driving back the savages and in stemming the tide of the American Revolution. Whatever may have been their faults, their virtues were such that Gaston County, the State, and Nation have greatly benefited by their contribution.

THE GERMANS

The Germans, many of whom came to Gaston County about the same time or, as the weight of evidence seems to show, a little later than the Scotch-Irish, were also from Pennsylvania where they first landed. Some few Germans came to this country with the Swedish and Dutch settlers, but it was not until the founding of Pennsylvania that any considerable numbers arrived. Their migrations to America have been divided into three well-defined periods. The first was from 1663 to about 1709. During that time a few came to Pennsylvania each year. The Palatines (Calvinists) came during the second period, 1709 to 1727. Thousands of them, in consequence of the ravaging of the Palatinate by war and the prevailing religious and economic tyranny, took refuge in England in 1709 with the hope that Queen Anne would send them to America. The English government sent some to the Carolinas, many to New York. A few hundred eventually found their way into Pennsylvania. About 1710 the Palatines began to come with Swiss settlers directly to Pennsylvania. By the close of the second period, the number of Germans alone in the Pennsylvania colony has been estimated as between fifteen and twenty thousand.

During the third period, 1727 to 1775, the number of immigrants reached enormous proportions. Most of the Germans coming to North Carolina were first a part of the Pennsylvania colony. An estimate of the number, based upon the lists of arrivals passing through the port of Philadelphia, gives an aggregate of nearly seventy thousand, about one-half of whom arrived within the six years, 1749 to 1754. Authorities agree that at the outbreak of the Revolution they comprised about one-third of Pennsylvania's population.

While many stayed and their descendants are still living in Pennsylvania, numbers of others left that state to scatter over North Carolina where they helped to build, in a favorably situated section, another great commonwealth. Most of them had come over during the third period of migration, and from 1740 to 1745 took the "Great Road" through York and Lancaster Counties, Pennsylvania, the Shenandoah valley and across the Dan, and scattered over the state. Many came into Piedmont Carolina and into what is now Gaston County by the same route as the Scotch-Irish.

They came in canvas-covered wagons, low in front and high behind where a feed trough was placed. Pots, pans, water buckets, and many other necessary articles dangled within easy reach when camp was made. Within were household goods, food and clothing, farm tools, and white-haired, rosy cheeked children looking from behind the covers, in wide-eyed amazement, at the strange sights they beheld. Two or more horses drew the wagons. Extra ones were used by the women for riding. A drove of cows, pigs, and sheep, rounded up by the men and boys and a dog, usually constituted the caravan. Their worldly possessions were few, but about the only capital needed for the development of the good lands which they found was thrift, energy, and common sense, all of which the Germans had in abundance.

So it is readily seen that various motives prompted the migrations of the German settlers who came into America from Europe. Some were moved by religious zeal as well as a desire to establish for themselves homes in the wilderness. Others were anxious to get away from the terrible civil wars carried on in the interest of their rulers in which they frequently lost the earnings of years. They believed that on the vast continent beyond the seas war would trouble them no more, and that they would find a place where they could worship God as they pleased. But alas! A few years after their arrival, they, with their Scotch-Irish and a few English neighbors who were then in this country, were plunged into the maelstrom of the Revolution where they did valiant service in the cause of American freedom.

The Germans were a law-abiding, fun-loving people. Their interest in Easter celebrations and Kris Kringle merrymakings is still evident in their descendants. As a farmer, the German was industrious and thrifty. His farm was usually small but well kept; his cattle fat and glossy. His greatest asset was his ability to produce what was needed both in food and material for clothing.

The custom of the Germans in coming in congregations and settling in communities gave them a decided advantage over others who settled on widely scattered farms in that their social, educational, and religious life was more readily developed. The schoolhouses were crude, but the teachers were often men of ability who were sent from Pennsylvania or Germany. For many years the text books used in the schools were written in the German language. Not until after the Revolution was English taught in the German schools. The older settlers opposed this reform and clung to the language of their childhood. But their children, finding themselves in a community where all transactions were carried on in the English tongue, naturally desired a change. English took the place of German not only in the schools but in the daily affairs of the settlers until their names, in many cases, became Anglicized.

The educational thought of the county has been and is influenced by the Germans. Their share in the industrial development is striking and important because they brought with them from Germany a love for and knowledge of this industry.

The German citizenry of the county has been a conservative, steadying influence of much value. Mr. Hoffman in "Our Kin" said of them: "I do not claim that these good old people whose memories I am trying to preserve were great in worldly pomp or show or brilliant achievement. They were just good honest people, contented to establish families in the wilderness and support them from agriculture, mechanical or other manual pursuits; but I do claim: They were great in their endurance and patience, their strong common sense, industry and frugality, and their rugged adherence to duty as they saw it. In all the homely virtues of life they were great."

The dates of setting off frontier counties show the progress of emigration and increase of population, but do not fix the time of establishment of settlements; neither do the dates of land patents mark the time because the lands were sometimes occupied a long period before grants were made and the lands surveyed. At other times patents were granted before emigration.

The part of Anson County which is now Mecklenburg was settled almost wholly by the Scotch and Scotch-Irish. The Germans desiring their own countrymen for neighbors passed by the Scotch-Irish and crossed the Catawba River. They took possession of the northern part of the present County of Gaston. Their settlements were for the most part north of an imaginary line running westward from the Catawba River across the county and beginning just south of Dutchman's Creek. There they founded compact communities with a church and school the center of each. The same building was often used for both, and the minister was usually the teacher.

While most of the pioneers who came to Gaston
County were Scotch-Irish and German, there were a
few English and other nationalities who had formed
ties with them by marriage or sometimes only by
association. English traders from the colonies of
Virginia came early among the Indians and first
white settlers. Some of them stayed and became a
part of the settlements. But not many English were
here until after the Revolutionary War when they,
too, began buying and occupying lands along the
Catawba and pushing up its tributary streams.
Though this is true, it is known that among them
were many who tarried for awhile and then moved
on farther west. The reason for this is not known.
It may have been the antagonism of the Scotch-Irish
caused by the enmity that continued to burn because
of their treatment by the English while in Ireland,
and which had not entirely spent itself.

The third stream of emigration, which flowed
from Africa, did not spread over the present Gaston
County for a long time after it reached American
shores. Old wills show that a few negroes were
among the pioneers, but it was not until about 1830,
when the raising of cotton began taking its place as
one of our principal industries, that they were here
in any appreciable numbers. The Negro was later
to become an important factor in the industrial life
of the county.

REASONS FOR COMING

When pioneers enter a new country and stay to
build permanent homes, they are influenced by some

existing condition or conditions. In Gaston County and adjacent territory, they were induced to settle on account of the inviting nature of the climate and soil, the many streams and clear bold springs, and the comparative quietness of the Catawba Indians. They passed by the vacant lands of Virginia, near the settlements there, because of the severity of Virginia laws on the subject of religion in comparison with those of the Carolinas. The Virginia settlers were expected to conform to the Church of England.

The presence of pasturage was another influencing condition which encouraged and directed emigration in its early periods. Vast prairies, covered with pea vine grass and cane brakes, stretched across Virginia and North Carolina where large forests later grew. The grass-covered prairies abounded with game and supplied grazing land, in both winter and summer, for the stock which the settlers brought with them and which was, at first, a principal source of wealth.

The Catawba River bottoms which were not planted in Indian maize were prairie, as were other large areas of the county. This fact has been established by reliable tradition. Mrs. Elizabeth Gullick Caldwell, widow of Samuel Caldwell, a Revolutionary soldier, who lived on the site of Belmont Abbey College, told Mrs. Elizabeth Hall that the land in front of and adjoining her home place, now owned by the estate of the late Kelly Kee, was prairie. Colonel Richard Rankin, son of William

Rankin, another Revolutionary soldier, attested the truth of the prairie tradition. He stated that the horses were turned loose on Saturday afternoons in the high grass and that the tingling of the bells enabled their owners to find them on Monday mornings when they were needed for work.

While prairies abounded, there was also much woodland which supplied logs for the first rude cabins, fuel that kept the settlers warm, and materials for furniture, farm tools, and other necessary things.

The pioneers found here, in Gaston County, even at that remote date a goodly land, "a land flowing with milk and honey."

The Germans: . . . About the only capital needed for the development of the good lands which they found was thrift, energy, and common sense, all of which the Germans had in abundance.

CHAPTER IV

As early as 1740, the log cabins of the pioneer Scotch-Irish were taking the places of the Indian tepees along both sides of the Catawba River, but not until about ten years later did family records and deeds and grants, a few dating back to the time when Gaston County was a part of Anson or Bladen, begin to throw light upon the first settlers. In those records were given their names, the location of the land, though often indefinite, the date of entry, the date of grant, and the acreage. The pioneers soon pushed up the tributary streams. Water courses and rich bottom lands determined many places of settlement. Their homes were usually built on bluffs overlooking the streams. Soon they were scattered over that part of the county south of Dutchman's Creek. The home sites of families of Ulster Scots, called Scotch-Irish, whose names were later glorified at Ramseur's Mill and King's Mountain, may still be pointed out. Usually there is nothing left but a few scattered stones which were part of a chimney.

An occasional land grant or patent has been, and is yet, in possession of a family in the county. As a rule the locations of those tracts are accurately described, but many, in the office of the Secretary of State, are so uncertainly defined that many disputes and lawsuits have resulted.

Some of the grants recorded in Raleigh were issued about 1750, a few before that time, and many from 1750 to the Revolutionary period. A few Germans, Highland Scotch, and English mingled with the Scotch-Irish in the southern part of the county, but not many Highland Scotch have ever come and the English who remained to become a part of the permanent settlements were scarce until after the Revolutionary War.

While this is true, among the first recorded comers was a mixture of nationalities who settled in the Point, so called from the neck of land jutting out into the water at the confluence of the South Fork and Catawba Rivers. Among them were Frederick Hambright, German; the Hardins, Hambright's brothers-in-law, English; Robert Leeper, English; James Kuykendall, Dutch, who later settled on Dutchman's Creek which was named for him; Alexander McLean, Scotch-Irish; and doubtless many others; but those named will give an idea of the mixture in that particular locality.

In the early fifties, many entries were made and grants issued. The records show that the Scotch-Irish were a thrifty people of whom it is said that "they keep the Sabbath and everything else they get their hands on," which accusation was not as true as that they were shrewd enough to enter large tracts of land or, as is often recorded, several tracts in different sections of a territory. Then, as the old deeds show, they sold to other pioneers who came in, and moved from one place to another. This seems to have been the reason there were not as

many well-established homes among the Scotch-
Irish as among the Germans.

Robert Leeper was one of the first known settlers
near the junction of the rivers. His earliest grant for
350 acres was issued March 31, 1750. Therefore it
is known that he was here before that time. During
the succeeding five years, he obtained other grants
in the same locality which gave him a large acreage.
In addition he acquired tracts in other parts of the
county.

James Kuykendall, an associate of Robert Leeper,
came about the same time. He was granted much
land over the county. His first recorded grant for
600 acres was entered September 28, 1750, and
issued April 1, 1751. It was also near the junction
of the rivers.

For one or two years, according to the records,
the families of Robert Leeper and James Kuykendall had the Point section almost entirely to themselves, except for the Indians. One grant earlier
than those of Leeper and Kuykendall, issued to
Thomas Robertson, was in the Point, dated April
13, 1749. Another was issued to Thomas Potts in
1750.

At that time the peaceful nature of the Catawba
Indians was not understood. The white people had
not been here long enough to know that, though
they sometimes robbed, they rarely ever killed a
white. But the Cherokees were a hostile tribe and
often raided the Catawba territory, plundering and
occasionally committing murder. As a protection
from Catawba, Cherokee, or both, a fort and stock-

ade were built by Robert Leeper, James Kuykendall, and two others whose names are not known, at the junction of the South Fork and Catawba Rivers. The fort was rudely constructed of logs at the foot of a bluff from which a bold spring flowed. This bluff is now covered by the waters of the Duke Power development. It was on the left bank of the South Fork near a neck of land called the Point where the rivers meet.

The building was within an enclosure, triangular in shape, formed by a stockade on one side which began at the Catawba and ended at a point on the Fork. The rivers formed the other two sides of the triangle.

The site of the fort was ideal and made such an appeal to Leeper, Kuykendall, and the few others who first saw it that it likely helped determine their place of settlement. Later, many were attracted to the locality by the protection offered. Among the number was Frederick Hambright. With him were his wife and children and his wife's brothers, the Hardins.

Hambright had several grants. The earliest was dated August 30, 1753. William Haggerty had a grant bearing the same date, indicating a friendship between the two men.

Others holding early grants in the same section were: Robert Palmer, Robert Patterson, Robert Patrick, William Patten, Rachel Price, Robert Ramsey, George Penick, James Sharpe, David Templeton, John Thomas, John Turner, William Barnett, and Edward Boyle.

By 1753 many had settled in the southern part of the county. From that time, for two or three years, grants were issued in rapid succession. The land was rich, the Indians were comparatively quiet, and the fort was there, a place to flee for safety in case of trouble. The outlook was promising and large numbers came. Some remained to help build a community; others sought even fairer fields in other places, their names to be forgotten in the place of their once habitation. Among them were the Coburns, John, Judith, and Samuel, who were evidently located before that time, 1753, since Samuel Coburn commanded a company, at least some of whom were Gaston County men, in the Spanish Alarm. These were George Cathey, Thomas Walker, John Watkins, William Dicky, Margaret Dicky, James Harris, William Henry, Charles Mc-Knight, William McKnight, Samuel Neely, Robert McClenachan, Thomas Leonard, the Allisons, and many others.

In addition there were many purely Scotch or Scotch-Irish names, the location of whose grants is quite uncertain. The only definite thing about most of them is that they were on the Catawba River.

The bottom lands of the Catawba being soon taken, the settlers began pushing up the South Fork and its tributaries. Among the lower South Fork pioneers were James Hemphill, James Spratt, and John Clark who likely moved across the river to found the Mecklenburg family of Clarks. John Armstrong was the pioneer of his name in lower Gaston. He obtained a grant dated August 30,

1753, for 350 acres on the Belmont side of Armstrong's ford, now Armstrong's bridge. On the same date, James Armstrong was granted 229 acres on Beaver Dam Creek. He obtained other grants in the northern part of the county; then, two years later, one on the South Fork near that of John. He had as many as six tracts in different parts of the county from Beaver Dam Creek to the Catawba River. Martin was another Armstrong who early settled on the Fork.

There were other settlers in various parts of the county. William Barnett owned as many as four tracts of land between the rivers. The earliest of his grants was dated March 31, 1753. The father of Major Chronicle purchased from William Barnett the land on which he lived and on which the town of Belmont is now located. Samuel Wilkins, as early as 1751, owned a thousand acres on the South Fork. James Wilson owned 1070 acres in several tracts on the South Fork. John Sloan owned land on Little Long Creek, Indian Creek, and other places. He obtained considerable land in Mecklenburg about the time that county was formed and moved his place of residence there. Robert Sloan, a brother of John, also had several grants on the east side of the river. Robert later gave his life for his country at Ramseur's Mill, while leading a company of militia at that place.

There is a record of a Giles Hicks having a grant of 320 acres on Beaver Dam Creek as early as 1735. If this is the Beaver Dam Creek in the upper part of the county, then this man was the first to ever own land in what is now Gaston County. There were no white people living here that early, but it is possible that a lone Indian trader or someone seeking pasturage for his cattle wandered in, became a squatter on the creek, and was granted a patent. The name Beaver Dam Creek would indicate that on it beavers built their dams. Christian Eaker was located on Beaver Dam Creek as early as 1755. Later he had a grant on Long Creek, and Peter Eaker, in 1761, had grants on both sides of Indian Creek.

The first Gullick mentioned in the county was John or Jonathan, who secured land in 1756 on Catawba Creek. Jonathan married Margaret Baldriech Henry, the widow of Moses Henry, who was mortally wounded at King's Mountain. His sister, Elizabeth, married Sam Caldwell, also a King's Mountain hero.

William Chittim and Thomas Henry had grants on the South Fork in the early 1760's. They both sent sons to participate in the battle of King's Mountain.

On the 28th of March, 1754, Robert Patrick was granted 600 acres in the Point. Later he moved to what is now Belmont. There is now no trace of the home.

The late Mr. Miles Hoffman of Dallas, a descendant of German pioneers and author of "Our Kin," has done the people of the county an inestimable service in the collection and preservation of many facts about the German pioneers and others with whom they intermarried. Mr. Hoffman, shortly after this work was started, kindly gave the writer permission to use any of his material, which privilege is being freely taken advantage of. His efforts have enabled many to trace their genealogy through successive generations.

One, conceded to be the first or among the first of the German settlers, was Sebastian Best or Bess. The date of his coming is not known, but in Colonial Records of North Carolina, Vol. IV, p. 1039, among sundry petitions for warrants for land presented at a council held at the Council Chamber in New Bern the 7th day of April, 1750, was the following: "Bastian Best 400 Anson." It is not recorded that a patent for that entry was ever given, but one was granted to him dated May 15, 1754, and the land is described as "300 acres on the branches of Leeper's and Killian's creeks being the place where he now lives."

No positive dates of the pioneer Best could be found except those of the land petition, the patent, and his will, a copy of which may be seen in the will book in Mecklenburg County Court House. It is dated July 8, 1761, and states that at the time of making the will he lived on Dutch Buffalo Creek in the County of Anson. The will was evidently not recorded until after Mecklenburg was cut off from Anson County in 1762. Killian's and Leeper's Creeks form Dutchman's, then called Dutch Buffalo. The date of the will was only seven years after the land patent was granted, which would indicate that he died where he first settled and that it was his son, Bastian, Jr., who married Catherine, a daughter of

Peter Hoyle, and lived on the South Fork opposite the Peter Hoyle place. Bastian Best had numerous descendants; many of these, inheriting the pioneer spirit, moved west. This probably accounts for the fewness of the number now in the county.

The Hoyle or Heyl family also came early. They kept some records going back four generations before the Gaston pioneer, Peter, and his family left Germany. Peter was the son of Adam and Nancy Hoyle and was born May 14, 1710, near Weis Baden on the Rhine, in the district of Nassau, Germany. His wife, Catherine Dales, whom he married April 7, 1736, was born in the same Rhenish province, April 10, 1714. They landed at Philadelphia on September 11, 1738. (This date was obtained from the papers of Rev. Max H. Hoyle by his daughter, Mrs. Elizabeth Hoyle Rucker, of Charlotte, and verified by records in the Historical Society of Philadelphia.) They stayed in York, Pennsylvania, two years and then moved to Frederick, Maryland. After living there for seven years they came south in 1747 to what was then Bladen County, North Carolina, now Gaston. Their place of permanent settlement was on the South Fork at what was afterwards known as Hoyle's bridge, three miles from Dallas, on the road from Dallas to Stanley.

Peter Hoyle died November 1, 1781, and Catherine Dales Hoyle died April 7, 1787. They left several children, the oldest of whom was Jacob. Peter died without having made a will, and, according to English law, his estate went in its entirety to his oldest son, Jacob, and is so recorded in the Lincoln County records.

Adam Costner, or Kastner as the name was originally spelled, was the pioneer of another family coming into this section from the Rhine country of Germany by way of Pennsylvania. After dwelling there awhile, as did many others, they followed the wilderness road southward. Passing the settlements on the Yadkin, they crossed the Catawba and pressed on through the dense forests of the upper part of the county until they reached the South Fork, which they crossed, and established their home on the west bank of the river, a short distance below where Philadelphia Church stands near Freytag or Friday shoals.

In 1753 Jacob Costner, a son of the pioneer, obtained lands from the state by patent. There seems to be no record of a grant to Adam, though he is said to have owned large tracts in this one of the earliest settlements west of the South Fork River.

The first Lutheran church in the county, and the second of any faith, was near the Costner settlement. It was known as Kastner's Church, later Philadelphia. The earliest marked grave in the cemetery is that of Adam Costner, who died in 1767.

An early grant was also made to Philip Rudisill, a son of the common ancestor of the Rudisill family of the county. The location was between the Freytag or Friday shoals on a large tract of land containing 520 acres which extended from the river east-

ward across Hoyle's Creek. The grant was dated
May 20, 1754. Philip died in 1794 and is buried
in Philadelphia graveyard. He left a large family
of sons and daughters.

Still another emigrant was Jacob Rhyne. He
came from the German Palatinate and settled in
Gaston County. The name was variously spelled,
Rhyne, Rhine, Rine, and Rein. Jacob's will was
written in German. It was signed Jacob Rein, but
he called himself Jacob Rine. Many of his descendants still live and have become prominent in the
county.

Notice how the early settlers clung to Bible
names. Jacob Rhyne had a daughter named Magde-
lene, also called Eve, and fitly so, for she married
Adam Cloninger, or Kloninger, and became ancestress of the Cloninger family of the county. They
settled on upper Stanley Creek and lived out their
lives there. They lie buried in a private graveyard
near the old home.

A daughter of Adam and Eve Cloninger, also
named Eve, married George Hovis, the pioneer of
the family of that name. They settled on the west
side of the South Fork in the angle formed by the
river and Big and Little Long Creeks. His holdings
were extensive, reaching quite a distance up the
river and creeks.

Michael Rudisill, a brother of Philip, whose
home was near High Shoals on the South Fork,
was the first white man to settle in that section near
the present Lincoln-Gaston line on Leeper's Creek
where it joins Killian's and forms Dutchman's. He

was established there in 1750, in the heart of a dense wilderness peopled only by the Red Men. He and his family lived bravely with a people whose characteristics they did not know, but with a trust founded upon the belief that if kindness were shown it would be returned. Consequently they lived in peace and harmony with the Indians, and never once was their confidence betrayed.

The Rudisills were not long alone among the Indians. Others of their countrymen soon joined them; their settlements extended along both Leeper's and Killian's Creeks to their junction in the northeastern part of the county. Among the later comers was the Hoffman, or Huffman, family. The name of the pioneer is not known, but it is certain that he had six children, two sons and four daughters, who left many worthy descendants in this and adjoining counties.

Garret Wills or Wiltz was another member of the Dutchman's Creek colony. He owned much land there. The name has become extinct or nearly so in Gaston and adjacent territory, though there are many descendants of other names through the daughters.

The Cansler family, or Genseler which is the old German way of spelling the name, joined the Dutchman's Creek community sometime after it was founded, coming with other settlers from Pennsylvania. There has been some question about the nationality of this family, but Philip, the pioneer, and his son, Philip, left wills signing their names in German which seems to classify them.

Neither the Scotch-Irish nor the Germans were discouraged by the thoughts of an eighteenth century sea voyage which sometimes lasted for months and was filled with many discomforts and dangers and often death. Many emigrants died at sea as did both parents of the Lineberger brothers, Peter, Lewis, and John, the first of that name in the county. Their father and mother accompanied them from Germany. They landed first in England. The voyage from England was very stormy. The ship was driven on the ocean for eighteen months. Both parents of the adventurous young men died and were buried at sea. Gold and other valuables belonging to the family were lost. So they had nothing except strong arms and brave, but lonely, hearts with which to battle for existence in the wilderness; but America to them was a haven of refuge, a land of promise.

Romance and tradition cling 'round Pasour's Mountain, near Dallas. The peak was once called LaBoone because a man of that name and his wife once lived in a rock-walled cave on the mountain side. Stories have been told of neighborhood battles with Tories and of lonely graves. It is said that LaBoone was killed in a Loyalist-Tory skirmish and was buried by his father on the mountain. Later, the name was changed to Pasour's from the first settlers near it.

George Pasour or Bashore, as the name was then called, was the pioneer of the family and the first settler in that part of the county. He was nomadic in disposition, having entered several tracts of land.

He would enter a place, improve it, put up a cabin, plant a turnip patch, and then move on to enter another, leaving a son on the one vacated. He has many descendants. One of them is Mr. Sam Pasour whose son, George, lives with him on a farm which has been in the family for many years. The present home is a rambling farmhouse softened and greyed by the years. Near-by are the mouldering ruins of another home of the family whose members have long ago departed.

The principal book in the early German home was the Bible, treasured carefully on the ocean voyage and the wilderness journey. Copies may yet, occasionally, be seen among descendants of the pioneers. Mr. Pasour has a splendid example, still highly prized. It is a large book with wooden backs covered with beautifully tooled leather. The corners are brass, and there are the remains of two leather straps which doubtless held a lock, as old Bibles were often locked and chained to the desks. Mr. Pasour, now carrying the weight of years, sat on a bench and read from the Bible in the German language.

The pioneer Pasour was buried in a tiny cemetery on the side of the mountain near a small German Reformed Chapel which was afterwards burned. The burying ground was plowed up and its site lost.

Other German settlers in the neighborhood of Dallas were the Fronebergers. William was the family pioneer and was granted 202 acres of land on the north side of Long Creek on March 28,

1755, which would indicate that he was settled there before that time. He came from Germany as a Spencerian or writing teacher. After reaching North Carolina, he taught school in Cabarrus County and married a pupil by the name of Barringer. Soon after marriage, he and his bride moved to Gaston County and settled on Big Long Creek near LaBoone or Pasour's Mountain.

One son, as a soldier, married in Philadelphia and came to live with his father and mother. He reared a family of three sons and three daughters. Most, if not all, of the Fronebergers of the county are descended from him. Jacob, one of the number, married Mrs. Violet Pegram Holland, a daughter of Winchester Pegram, and was among the first settlers of Dallas. One of their children, Mrs. Elizabeth Froneberger Puett, still resides there. Many of the Froneberger descendants are still living near the old home place in the vicinity of Long Creek Presbyterian Church. A few of the names are Arrowwood, Ormand, and White.

The earliest of William Barnett's grants was dated March 31, 1753. The father of Major Chronicle purchased from William Barnett the land on which he lived and on which the town of Belmont is now located.

Gaston

Huffstetler

Reynolds

McKnight

Leonard

Crouse

Pioneer

Harris

Coburn

Kiser

McElmurry

Baker

Friday

Families

Walker

HARDIN

Carpenter

Dicky

HEMPHILL

McCullocks

Price

Ewing

Alexander

Moore

Scott

Dellinger

Chronicle

Torrence

Cathey

Aderholdt

Neely

McClenachan

Watkins

Penick

Plonk

CHAPTER V

ALEXANDER MCLEAN

The McLeans, among the original settlers of the Point, were numbered with the few who kept any family records. John McLean, Jr., a descendant of Alexander, the first McLean of the county, furnished material for this sketch. Alexander McLean was the progenitor of one of the Gaston County families of that name. Colonel Charles McLean headed another and became prominent as a civil and military leader. So far as it is known, he was not related to the McLeans in the Point. If a relationship existed at all, it was distant.

Alexander McLean was born in Scotland or on the Isle of Mull, one of the numerous islands off the western shore. His mother died the night he was born, and his father moved to the County of Antrim, Ireland, where he married again. Between 1725 and 1730 Alexander sailed from Antrim to America, landing at Philadelphia. He had no earthly possessions except a certificate of membership in the Presbyterian Church of Ireland. Having no money to pay the expenses of the voyage, he hired himself to an Englishman, named Ratchford, who lived in Dublin and was coming over on the same boat, for the amount necessary for the trip. He promised to discharge the debt afterwards by working for him. At the age of thirty, when he had laid up several hundred dollars, he married Elizabeth Ratchford, daughter of his former benefactor. They remained some years in Pennsylvania where three children, Jean, Margaret, and Agnes were born. Two of these died of smallpox.

After leaving Pennsylvania, the family came to Rowan County and settled in the Dobbin neighborhood, eight miles from Salisbury. Here a son, John, was born and about one year later, April 2, 1757, their son William was born. He was to become one of Gaston's foremost citizens. Soon after the birth of William, Alexander McLean moved from his home near Salisbury to a tract of land close by the junction of the South Fork and Catawba Rivers, where three other sons, Alexander, George, and Thomas were born. He and his wife were consistent members of the Presbyterian church and lived to a good old age. His wife survived him a few years. Both are buried in the old Smith graveyard near Belmont.

JOHN GLENN

John Glenn and his first wife, Elizabeth Spratt, came to this country from the north of Ireland some time prior to 1755. Before coming to this section, he took part in Braddock's defeat and later settled in what was then Tryon and now Gaston County. His first known place of residence was the Becky Matthews farm near Lowell. He lost his first wife and then married Jean, or Jane, McLean, daughter of Alexander McLean and sister of Dr. William McLean. After his second marriage, circumstances would indicate that he changed his place of residence to a home nearer the McLean lands, since, as is recorded, he became road overseer for the Armstrong's Ford-South Carolina road.

After the death of Jane McLean, he married a Miss Grissom. He lived to be a hundred and one years old. A lone tombstone marks his grave near the center of old Goshen Cemetery.

JAMES LEEPER

James Leeper was one of the Catawba River pioneers. The date of his settlement is not known, but a grant to him from King George III was enrolled in the general office in Wilmington on the 8th day of April, 1765. It was for a tract of land containing 300 acres lying on the west side of the river in what is now Gaston County, of our Province of North Carolina, joining his own plantation on beginning. The survey and plot were made by McKnitt Alexander, a signer of the Mecklenburg Declaration of Independence. The above proves that James Leeper owned a plantation and was living on the Catawba before the grant was made.

An older grant in the same locality was one of the many to Frederick Hambright. It was dated April 23, 1762, and joined the west side of the Catawba River. It was near the James Leeper land and was later sold by Hambright to him.

James Leeper also bought from William McElmurry, another Catawba River settler, 200 acres which he had obtained by patent in 1762.

NICHOLAS LEEPER

Nicholas Leeper, a nephew of Robert Leeper, came to the Point several years later than his uncle. There is a record that he obtained a grant on April 23, 1762, for 190 acres on the Catawba River. The date is the same as that on which Frederick Hambright was granted the land he afterwards sold to James Leeper.

The location of the Nicholas Leeper grant and the one purchased by James Leeper from Frederick Hambright would make the two Leepers close neighbors. Both the Leeper and Hambright grants are now in possession of the writer, the lands having been purchased by her father, the late C. T. Stowe.

Nothing is known of Robert Leeper's family, if he had one. James, the nephew of Robert, was the father of Matthew, the Revolutionary soldier. Nicholas was the ancestor of many of the name now living in the Point.

FREDERICK HAMBRIGHT

Frederick Hambright, a pioneer, whose name was to add renown to the annals of the county, was born in Germany in 1727. He emigrated to Pennsylvania and from there he came to Virginia. Later, at a time not definitely known, he came to what is now Gaston County.

His first recorded land grant was not in the German communities north of Dutchman's Creek, but near the fort built by Robert Leeper, James Kuykendall, and others at the junction of the South Fork and Catawba Rivers. The patent is described as "on the south side of the Catawba River, adjoining Judith Coburn's survey in Anson County." It is dated August 30, 1753.

On April 23, 1762, another tract of 150 acres was granted to him by King George III on the west bank of the Catawba. Later, that tract was sold to James Leeper and became a part of what is known in South Point Township as the Leeper land. The original grant to Frederick Hambright and plot of survey, made by Francis Beaty, District Surveyor, are now in possession of the writer. On September 24, 1764, he patented land in the German territory between Stanley and Mt. Holly. In May, 1769, another tract was granted to him between the fork of Long Creek and a branch known as Still House Branch near Dallas. On this land he had built a cabin, and here he was living at the time of the battle of King's Mountain.

He was accompanied from Virginia by his brothers-in-law, Colonel Joseph Hardin, John and Benjamin Hardin; James Kuykendall, who later settled near the mouth of Dutchman's Creek; Nathaniel Henderson; Robert Leeper; and others.

As Lieutenant Colonel Hambright, he did valiant service in the Revolution, taking a prominent part in the battle of King's Mountain.

His Revolutionary record will be given in another sketch.

ANTHONY ALLISON

The Allisons were among the first settlers in the Point section. Andrew was the pioneer of the name.

It is recorded that he was granted 640 acres of land, April 3, 1752. Two of the family, John and James, likely sons of Andrew, were Revolutionary soldiers and were later pensioned, as is stated in Colonial Records. Another, Anthony, was head of a family when the first census was taken in 1790. At that time he had one son under sixteen and three females in the family, probably two little girls and their mother.

Anthony was the father of James Allison, who married Sallie Ewing, a daughter of Hugh Ewing, Revolutionary patriot. Anthony lived on the farm later owned by the late Captain John Smith. The Smith house is still standing, a short distance from the South Point road. Anthony Allison and members of his family were buried on the place near the present home of the Misses Emma and Mary Jane Bowen. Captain Smith, during his life, built and kept an enclosure around the graves. He was interested because his sister, Nancy Smith, married Green Allison, a son of Anthony.

Anthony Allison was said to have been a man of wealth, which was evidenced later in the home of two granddaughters, Lizzie and Martha Allison, who were for many years unique characters in the Belmont community. With these two women the childish memories of the writer are pleasantly associated. They lived between Belmont and the Catawba River with their mother, "Aunt Sallie" Ewing Allison, and their brother John and his family. The home was an unpretentious, weather-beaten house, containing many objects of beauty, such as rare china and charming pieces of antique furniture placed here and there, showing that the family had once been of prominence. Many flowers filled the yard and garden, spilling over the hillside on which the house was situated and extending down to the big rock-walled spring and branch at the foot of the slope. Having been taken there often as a child, the quaint beauty of the place was absorbed and is still a fragrant memory to the writer. Nothing now remains to mark the site of a once interesting home.

The Ewing, Allison, and Charles McLean families were closely associated, which leads to the belief that the Allisons of Allison Creek were of the same family as those of Gaston County. Likely all were of the Philadelphia Allisons. See sketch of Charles McLean.

THE BLACKS OF CHERRYVILLE

Among the pioneers of the northern part of the county were the Blacks of Cherryville. They were of Scotch-Irish origin and came with many of their countrymen to America, first settling in Pennsylvania. At least four members of the family, David, Thomas, John, and William, all brothers with the possible exception of David who may have been their father, made their way to North Carolina.

After wandering about for awhile, Thomas, the progenitor of the Cherryville Blacks, reached that section and purchased some land on November 23, 1762. The records show that this land was located on the south side of Indian Creek, a few miles out from Cherryville, and joined a 370 acre tract bought the same day and from the same party by Valentine Mauney, a brother of Christian Mauney, the ancestor of Mr. S. S. Mauney and others of Cherryville. Thomas Black, two or three years later, bought more land beyond Shelby to which he moved his family. Here he made his home until the time of his death in 1779.

Ephriam, a son of Thomas Black, moved back to the vicinity of Indian Creek, probably to the same land his father had owned. While living here, Ephriam Black bought the land on which Cherryville now stands and divided it between two of his sons, Steve and Thomas. They built their homes on the "Old Post Road," a small part of which may still be traced in the town. Long after the Blacks lived there, it was called "Cherry Lane" because Steve Black and his wife set out many cherry trees in the fence corners along the way. From this fact Cherryville received its name.

THE MAUNEYS AND THEIR NEIGHBORS

Among others to settle in the Cherryville section were the Mauneys and their neighbors.

There were three Mauney brothers, Christian, Valentine, and Jacob. The earliest records of them are in land grants and deeds. The first date on which mention of one of them was made was in a deed conveying to Valentine Mauney 370 acres on the north side of Indian Creek. This was on November 3, 1762, in consideration of five shillings. On April 19, 1763, Jacob received a royal grant for 300 acres. Five years later, on April 28,

1768, Christian Mauney was granted 200 acres, and on December 8, 1770, he purchased 350 acres on Beaver Dam Creek near the Peter Eaker settlement. On the lands of this purchase Christian Mauney made his home. He is the one to whom most of the present generation of Mauneys of this section trace their origin. In the neighborhood of their first settlement in the county, Christian and Valentine lived out their lives and here they lie buried. Christian is buried in the old Beaver Dam Cemetery near Crouse, and Valentine in Antioch Cemetery between Crouse and Cherryville. It is not known what became of Jacob. The names of Valentine Mauney and Jacob Mauney, Jr., perhaps a son of the older Jacob, were signed to the Tryon County Declaration of Independence. Christian's name, for some reason, was omitted.

Other pioneers of the Cherryville section, neighbors of the Mauneys, bore names well known at the present time, such as: Carpenter, Crouse, Dellinger, Huffstetler, Reynolds, Rudisill, Kiser, Plonk, Aderholdt, Baker, Friday or Fretag, Black, Eaker, and many others who came, for the most part, from the forests of Germany.

GEORGE RUTLEDGE

Some interesting old grants were in possession of the late Mrs. W. B. Rutledge and her daughter, Mrs. Annie Rutledge Rollins of Mt. Holly. The name is also spelled Routhlege or Routlege and appears to be English. It is likely one of the few

English families among the pioneers who stayed. Many others pushed on toward the West.

The first of the Rutledge grants was from King George II to George Rutledge, the pioneer, for lands lying in then Anson County. It was dated 1753, and joined the lands of James Kuykendall, the first to obtain a grant in the Mt. Holly section. A second grant was given the same George Rutledge for 320 acres on Kuykendall's Creek, later called Dutchman's, because Kuykendall was a Dutchman from Holland, who had affiliated himself with the Scotch-Irish. This grant was dated Anson County, May 20, 1754, and is recorded in the office of the Secretary of State. Many others known to exist are not recorded there.

A grant was also given to James Armstrong in 1753. He deeded it to Joseph Armstrong. Joseph sold it to George Rutledge in 1754.

Just prior to the 1750's, George Rutledge served in the Spanish Alarm, an uprising of Spanish allies and Indians who came up from Florida to overcome the English and take possession of the Carolinas. He was a member of Captain Samuel Coburn's Company, which helped protect the frontiers.

He died in 1779.

SAMUEL WILSON

One of the earliest settlers in the Crowder's Mountain section of Gaston County was Samuel Wilson. He was one of that great Scotch population who sojourned for a period in Ireland, making his home in Belfast. Being of an adventurous nature, in the fall of 1767 he boarded an Irish trading ship for Charleston, South Carolina. He was accompanied by his wife and five children.

He secured his passage on the ship by mortgaging to the ship's owner a land grant from King George III. The mortgage was not expected to be cancelled, as mortgages of this type were taken to encourage immigration. Consequently he lost the grant, but land was so plentiful that it was an easy matter to obtain title to other tracts.

The Wilsons landed safely in Charleston and settled on lands offered by the Province of South Carolina to Protestant settlers.

Following, perhaps, the urge of adventure once more, Samuel Wilson soon left his Protestant lands and came, before the Revolution, to a thickly wooded and almost uninhabited region of Gaston County, near Crowder's Mountain.

Samuel Wilson left many descendants. Thomas Wilson, the youngest child, was the forbear of many of that name now living in this section. He married Jane Whitesides and settled near Pisgah Church, not far from the spot where his father located.

The Wilsons, of sturdy pioneer stock, have made valuable contributions to the life, development, and growth of Gaston County.

SAMUEL RANKIN

Samuel Rankin, the Gaston County pioneer of the family of that name, was of Scotch-Irish stock.

He, with the Moores, Alexanders, and others of his countrymen, came to the Mt. Holly section from Pennsylvania about 1763 and settled on Kuykendall or Dutchman's Creek on lands opened by the government a short time before, some of which had been taken by James Armstrong. The lands of Samuel Rankin's first settlement were purchased from Armstrong. Two years later he moved to a large grant of 2000 acres, lying between Stanley and Dutchman's Creeks.

While living in Pennsylvania, he married Ellen Alexander, a sister of Robert Alexander and an aunt of Margaret Alexander, Robert's daughter, who was betrothed to Major William Chronicle at the time of his death at King's Mountain. Robert Alexander also moved to the Mt. Holly section and became prominent in the county.

Samuel Rankin and his wife had eleven children. One of these, William, was a soldier of the Revolution. A sketch of him will be given later.

Much of the land of the original grant to Samuel Rankin is still in possession of his descendants. The late Rufus Rankin, reared in the New Hope section of the county, built a new house on the site of the original settlement, about two miles from Stanley on the north side of Stanley Creek. Rufus died a short time after his home was completed. His widow, Minnie Armstrong Rankin, continued to occupy it for a while, but she later moved to Gastonia.

The settlement has for years been known as Rankintown.

NATHANIEL ELDRIDGE

Mrs. C. P. Robinson of Olney and Mrs. S. A. Robinson of Gastonia have in their possession some interesting old papers which throw much light on some of the first settlers of the Crowder's Creek section. Many names are given: those to whom deeds were made, owners of adjoining lands, surveyors, chain bearers, and others. The oldest of these papers, in possession of Mrs. S. A. Robinson, is a grant signed by William Tryon, Governor, and bearing the seal of King George III. The grant was issued on the 27th day of April, 1767, to Nathaniel Eldridge and was for 300 acres of land on a branch of Crowder's Creek. Attached to the grant is a plot of the land with boundaries. The survey began with a red oak on Alexander Robinson's line.

Nathaniel Eldridge later bought another tract from the State. It adjoined what he already had and the lands formerly belonging to James Scott. Part of one patent granted to Eldridge for land adjoining that of Hugh Torrence was conveyed by him to John Massey, by John Massey to Isaac Davis, by Isaac Davis to Elisha Cox, by Elisha Cox to Thomas Berry, and by Thomas Berry to James Robinson. Other names mentioned, who were early settlers, were: Robert, William, and David McCullocks, John Robinson, David and Joseph Robinson, Hugh Torrence, and others.

ALEXANDER ROBINSON

Another pioneer in the Crowder's Creek section was Alexander Robinson. The exact time of his location is not known, but, as the Eldridge survey began on his line, it is known that he was settled there before the Eldridge grant was given. He was the ancestor of the Robinsons of Union, Gastonia, and other places who have made valuable contribution to the growth and upbuilding of the county.

The name is variously spelled Robinson, Robeson, Robertson, Robson, and Roberson; but all are the same family name. Families often had to change the spelling of their name to conform to that of the clerk or secretary on deeds or grants to make them good. This accounts, in a way, for the diverse spellings of many family names.

JAMES HENDERSON

One of the most picturesquely located towns in Gaston County is McAdenville on the west bank of the South Fork at the great shoals. On the east bank rise rugged and precipitous hills, lapped by the singing waters of the river. One hill reaches a height of 150 feet. On this cliff, surrounded by loved ones, repose the remains of two former owners of the shoals, James Henderson and Adam Alexander Springs. James Henderson, before the Revolutionary War, obtained a great tract of land here, including the shoals. He erected at the base of a hill a flour and grist mill which was turned by the magnificent water power. Running a mill of this type was a leading enterprise in the early days, and remained so until the marvelous development of the cotton mill industry. Henderson's mill was three stories high. His residence was in the third story which he entered from the hill.

Not much is known of the life of James Henderson except that he was of a Scottish family, that he married Violet Lawson, a daughter of Hugh Lawson, and that he was a Revolutionary soldier.

ADAM ALEXANDER SPRINGS

In the beginning of the last century, the shoals and Henderson estate passed to John Springs, who within a few years transferred it to his son, Adam Alexander Springs. The "Henderson Shoals" then became known as the "Springs Shoals." Adam A. Springs was an honor graduate in the first class to complete its courses at the University of North Carolina, in 1798. His will, a quaint document, explains the little graveyard on the top of the hill. It is written thus: "In the first place, I will to be buried alongside of James Henderson on the hill on the east of the shoals, formerly called 'Henderson Shoals', and then I wish my executors to build or cause to be built a stone fence leaving James Henderson and myself at a beginning corner, the fence to be thirty feet square; the balance of this square will be a family burying place at these shoals, formerly called the 'Henderson Shoals'. As to my grave, I leave that to the modest discretion of my executors."

His request was carried out and a monument erected with the following inscription: "Sacred to the memory of Adam Alexander Springs who was born on the 9th day of January, 1776, and departed this life on the 8th day of April, 1840."

There is a tradition that Adam Springs was buried standing up so that he could watch his fish traps and, perhaps, the beautiful panorama of hills and stream before him.

Some stones, without inscription, and the stump of a large tree are the only markers of the grave of James Henderson, but the Springs grave gives its location. After a laborious climb the little graveyard, with its massive walls now tumbling down, can be found and the grave of Springs, plainly marked. The reclining stone broken in many places and the hand-wrought iron gate swinging in the breeze make the place seem lonely and forgotten. If these two pioneers could hear, they would know that the hum of the spindle and the note of the loom are vying with nature's cadence, the musical voice of the river.

REV. HUMPHREY HUNTER

Near Londonderry, in the northern part of Ireland, on May 14, 1754, was born a man destined to play an important part in the life of Gaston County, the Rev. Humphrey Hunter.

His father died when he was a small child. A few months later, when the boy was about five years old, he accompanied his mother and several brothers and sisters to America. After a long voyage, they arrived at Charleston, August 27, 1759. From Charleston the journey was made by land to the neighborhood of Poplar Tent Presbyterian Church, where the widow bought land and spent the remainder of her life. Here she was joined, a few years later, by a married son, Henry, whom she had left behind in Ireland. We have no further notice of Humphrey Hunter until his presence, as a spectator, was noted in Charlotte, May 20, 1775, when his keen eye and quick brain enabled him to take in all that was done. He carried home a copy of the Mecklenburg Declaration of Independence and preserved it for many years.

Determined to have a classical education, he left the farm at twenty-three and entered Clio Nursery in 1778, under the Rev. James Hall. He remained there one year. After fighting Cherokee Indians for a while, he entered Queen's Museum, Charlotte. His stay there was brief, for in the summer of 1780 the school was closed on account of the march of Lord Cornwallis toward Charlotte. He then joined the army and was present at the battle of Camden where he was taken prisoner. After remaining in prison seven days, he, with many others, was taken to Orangeburg. From there he escaped and went home. Participation in the battle of Eutaw Springs ended his military career.

After that he began actively his preparation for the ministry and was licensed to preach, October 15, 1789.

In the fall of 1795 he came to Gaston County and was the first preacher to be regularly called to the pastorate of Goshen Church. He preached at both Goshen and Unity near the present Lincoln-Gaston line. These two congregations embraced all the territory on the west side of the Catawba River from above Beatty's ford to the South Carolina line and west from the river to the community of Olney Church, then in a flourishing condition.

The Rev. Humphrey Hunter purchased land and built a home on what is now a part of the plantation of the late Mr. Tom Springs, near Mt. Holly. The home site is a beautiful knoll plainly seen from Mr. Springs's yard. The house, so said Mr. Springs, was still there when he moved to the place thirty-odd years ago. At that time several of the old apple trees were still bearing fruit. The house site is plainly marked, the chimney being built on naturally imbedded granite which is plentiful all over the hill. Around the big house are the sites of the slave quarters. One slave, Ransom Hunter, is remembered by many of the older people of the Mt. Holly section.

The old highway from Charlotte to Lincolnton by way of the Tuckaseege ford passed near the house. The story is told that one Sunday morning two neighbors going along the way saw Mr. Hunter covering the top of an outbuilding. They inquired if he were not going to church. His reply was that he intended preaching tomorrow. He thought the day was Saturday. Imagine his chagrin when he found himself working on the Sabbath. Mr. Hunter was not only an eloquent preacher but also a thrifty, successful business man, doing much labor with his own hands.

The water supply for the home and farm came from a fine rock-walled spring. There was much rich bottom land on the creek near by, long known as Hunter's Creek.

After the hardships of his youth and young manhood, amidst quiet, peace, and plenty he shepherded his flock and brought up his family of ten children. One of these, Dr. Cyrus Lee Hunter, was the author of "Sketches of Western North Carolina" and contributor of rich earnings to the state in several branches of science. This son married Sophia Forney, the beautiful daughter of General Peter Forney. She is buried in Goshen graveyard.

Rev. Humphrey Hunter preached for thirty-eight years at Goshen, Unity, and Steele Creek. He died on the 21st day of August, 1827, and is buried at Steele Creek.

Over the hills and vales of his home place, which once rang with the songs of slaves and the laughter of little children, lie stillness and a faint blue haze.

ROBERT ARCHIBALD

Very near a bold spring, at the rear of Professor F. P. Hall's peach orchards, is an old house site, once the home of Robert Archibald, the first Presbyterian preacher ever to make his home in this section of Gaston County.

He was a man of education and culture, an orator of no mean ability. Nothing is known of him until his appearance in the graduating class of Princeton College in 1772. He was granted license to preach by Orange Presbytery in the fall of 1775. Three years later, October 7, 1778, he was ordained and installed pastor of Rocky River Church. It was between the years of licensure and his ordination that he lived at Belmont and preached at Goshen.

While Mr. Archibald was a gifted scholar, he was not a man of clearness of convictions. He first studied medicine; then he entered the ministry as a Presbyterian, afterward making several changes. Finally he became a Universalist. In 1794 Synod ordered the Presbytery of Orange to deal with him, with the result that he was suspended from the Presbyterian ministry and all churches were warned against him.

From the following conversation, said to have been held with a South Carolina woman, it would seem that one of his heresies was a belief in purgatory. She said to him, "D'ye think some folks will go to hell for a time then come out again?" "Yes, that's what I think." "And do you expect to go there yerself?" "Yes." "And how long do you expect to stay there?" "About fifteen years." "Ya'd be a pretty singed devil to come out, after being in so long," she said.

After his suspension from the Presbyterian ministry, he preached his Universalist doctrine wherever he could find an audience.

CHAPTER VI

IN COLONIAL DAYS

The manners and customs of the early Colonial period were necessarily crude and hard, but they should be of interest to those who would know how our remote ancestors lived and how those adventurous spirits fared in a new country without resources. Their lives furnish the vital spark which illuminates later history. By a study of the habits of a people who have played a principal role in its progressive development, we may better understand our country and its inhabitants, and it will enable us to have a more profound regard for the memory of those who blazed the trail and made possible our present civilization.

In addition to the more fortunate of the emigrants who came in wagons along the well-defined road from Pennsylvania through the Shenandoah valley, there was the average pioneer who moved into the new country on foot or on horseback and brought his few household goods on pack horses. When their destination was reached, the men and boys cut trees and constructed log houses. Each house was usually built on a hill overlooking a stream, near a spring of sparkling water. The first was of rude construction. Boards were split for the roof, which was held on by weight poles in the absence of nails. Floors and door shutters were made by splitting logs and hewing the flat side smooth. The chimneys were ordinarily of stone. The home sites of many pioneers may still be located by piles of chimney stones. The hearths were nearly always large flat rocks on which the family cooking was done by the women. This custom was kept up in many localities of what is now Gaston County until after the War between the States. When the cracks in the log walls were daubed with mud, the house was ready for occupancy, but there was no furniture. Rough bedsteads were constructed in the corners; and stools, benches, and tables were made. The rifle was hung over the door on pegs or the horns of bucks. One well-remembered home, built after the Reconstruction period, had three gun racks in the living room. Each gun was used for a different purpose on the farm. The hanging of the guns was one of many customs handed down from Colonial times, and showed how slowly changes were made until the great industrial development, beginning in Gaston County just prior to the War between the States, revolutionized them.

The windows in the first houses were few, and were merely openings with shutters and without glass. The doors were often in two sections; the upper part could be opened for air and light, while the lower section could be left closed. This arrangement also served the purpose of keeping small children indoors. Now, with a roof over their heads, with bedticks which they had brought along, filled with grass, and placed on the rudely constructed bedsteads, with pots, pans, and kettles from their precious supplies, with a big wide hearth of stone, and with piles of red-hot coals with which to cook their meagre fare, the immigrant was ready for other things.

Land had to be prepared for the first crop. Seeds for both field and garden and a few fruit trees had been brought along. Among the cherished possessions of the women were flower seeds, bulbs, and a few plants and shrubs, the progenitors of the old-fashioned flowers many of us remember in the gardens of our grandmothers.

After the first crop, things began to be a little easier. The land was rich and mellow and brought forth plentifully. Smoke from burning tracts of new ground could be seen constantly. Exhausted lands were never reclaimed, since it was easier to clear a new patch when more lands were needed. The men and boys, when not employed in the fields, spent much time hunting. This was profitable, as it helped supply the family larder. There was no time for idleness; more extensive fields needed to be cleared. If large trees were to be cut in a wooded section, neighbors were called in to help roll the logs in piles to be burned. When better homes took the place of the first rude cabins, neighbors were again called upon to assist in raising the walls. Log rollings, house raisings, and later quilting bees and corn shuckings were the main sources of amusement. The work was hard, but the good dinners, games, and fellowship of those with common interests were much enjoyed.

After the large trees were disposed of, either by girding or burning, the patch was fenced with rails, mostly of chestnut, split by the men of the family and boys old enough for such work.

Since the cattle roamed at will, it was necessary for every planter to put a fence around his cleared ground, except when some water course was sufficient to turn the animals, not only the domestic but also the wild ones that grazed on the grass-covered areas and roamed the forests. At that time deer were plentiful and remained so until about 1840.

Since, at first, there were no stores except those of English traders who kept only a few articles which white people wanted, the settlers were largely dependent upon their own resources. When the scant supplies brought with them began to wear out, the blacksmith built a forge on his own farm, where farming tools were repaired and replaced. Sheep and cattle were raised; the sheep furnished both food and clothing. Looms were set up in the attics and cloth was woven for many purposes, lovely examples of which have been handed down to the present time in the form of counterpanes, dresses, scarfs, and other things. Spinning wheels and reels were made. Cards for wool which had been brought from Philadelphia, or perhaps from the old country, were brought out. The hand mills, used at first for grinding wheat and corn, were replaced by mills erected on swift running streams. Tanneries were built on nearby creeks. Sawmills were set up and logs turned into planks.

Among the Scotch-Irish, about the only professions were the ministry, teaching, and surveying.

While it was necessary for all to farm, many trades were represented; and gradually skilled weavers, makers of barrels and casks, joiners, wheelwrights, wagon makers, tailors, blacksmiths, and others relieved the individual household of some of its tasks.

There were no schools at first. Boys and girls were expected to be hard working. Children were an industrial asset and large families were the rule.

The life of the pioneer woman was filled with many hard duties. She bore and reared large numbers of children, cooked for the family on the open hearth, dressed the skins of wild animals, milked the cows, churned the butter, and tended the calves, pigs, and chickens. She washed and ironed for the family, worked the garden, brought water from the spring, and carried milk and butter back and forth from the springhouse, sometimes a quarter of a mile away. The springhouse was the only available refrigerator. They made not only their own dresses but the materials as well. They spun the wool from their own sheep and later the cotton from their own patches into cloth, often going to the woods for roots and herbs from which they obtained dyes suitable to their own tastes. In addition, they made rugs and carpets.

For all this work, according to the old wills, the colonial husband, in grateful appreciation, usually lent (that's the word used) his widow a small portion of the family estate until she remarried or died.

Dipping tallow candles, by the flickering gleam of which colonial homes were lighted, was another of the numerous jobs of the pioneer housekeeper. At first strings suspended from a stick were dipped into a pot of melted tallow. As it cooled, it hardened around the strings. The dipping was repeated until the required thickness was reached. The invention of the candle mould eliminated much of this work.

Soap making was also done by the women. Behind each home an ash hopper was constructed of boards so placed in a trough as to form a triangular receptacle. This was filled with ashes from the hearth. When spring came and soap making time was near, water was poured on the ashes. As it soaked through, the ashes were leached and lye extracted, which ran out through the trough. In a big wash pot in the back yard, the lye was boiled with grease to form soap. The hot mixture, when ready, was poured into shallow vessels to cool; then it was cut into cakes. This custom was kept up in many homes until long after the War between the States.

Almost no cotton was raised during the Colonial period except a patch for family use. The seeds were picked out by hand, usually by the women and children before bedtime, while gathered round the evening torch. The cotton was then carded, spun, and knitted into stockings or woven into cloth.

The tanning of leather and the making of saddles, shoes, harness, and other articles necessarily became an important early industry. When the leather came from the tannery, it was dry and stiff and had to be treated with various solutions to soften and preserve it. Then it was dried and rolled with hand tools to remove the wrinkles. Usually there was a shoemaker in every community who took the measurements and made the shoes by hand. The harness maker was an important worker in leather during Colonial times, as the only means of traction was supplied by horses and oxen; therefore, sturdy harness for farm animals was much in demand. Since there were very few good roads, most traveling was done on horseback; so good saddles and bridles were necessary, and saddlers were never ranked among the unemployed.

Sleds, which could be made at home, were often used for drawing loads. There were almost no wagons in the settlements.

Before the women began the making of candles, the homes were lighted by pine knots or fat pitch pine, sometimes called candlewood, which was found plentifully everywhere in the forests. It was usually burned on a flat stone in one corner of the fireplace to avoid smoke and tar in the room.

Every family laid in a good supply of lightwood for winter use, even after the making of candles became customary. For a long time they were scarce and expensive and were often, in a spirit of frugality, extinguished during the long family prayers.

No industries have ever been more important than the iron and steel industries because machines upon which all other industries depend cannot be made without them. They add a great contribution to the comforts and conveniences of life. The Indians were existing under Stone Age conditions when the white man first came to America. He knew nothing of iron and was compelled to rely upon chipped flints for his axes and arrowheads. Mining became one of the earliest industries in what is now Gaston County. Iron ore was soon discovered, principally in the northern part of the county, and its mining became an early industry. It was not until the Revolutionary period that foundries were established and cast-iron articles were made.

Indian corn, a native of American soil, meant much to the pioneer. The Indians grew it plentifully on the bottom lands along the Catawba, the South Fork, and tributary streams. It helped to save the lives of the colonists and changed many of their methods of living and ways of cooking.

The settler soon learned that he had to turn to hunting, fishing, and planting for necessary food. He quickly acquired knowledge of how to grow corn successfully from its intelligent cultivation by the Indian. Corn became a staple article of food, and its culture became one of the most fruitful industries of the colonists.

Servants were few in the real pioneer days. The people did their own work, but as time wore on they grew more numerous and a few families owned slaves. When help was necessary in the average family, it was given by neighbors. Neighborliness was one of the firm rocks upon which the colonies grew. Assistance was furnished because of affectionate regard and could not be bought with current coin. The colonist turned to his neighbor for friendly advice in sickness, or death, or any emergency out of the ordinary. They lived in frequent everyday co-operation which was as necessary for progress as it had been in obtaining a foothold.

It was the spirit of neighborliness which helped to hold the colonists together and enabled them to overcome many of the obstacles and dangers of primitive existence. Finally, through their reliance upon each other and upon God, they gained their independence and were molded into a nation.

Another view of the colonial kitchen at Backcountry Farm, Schiele Museum, Gastonia. (Photo by Rick Haithcox Photography.)

Goshen Presbyterian Church, Gaston County's oldest, was organized in 1764. This building was replaced by the present brick church. *(Photo courtesy of the* Gaston Gazette.)

CHAPTER VII

GOSHEN CHURCH

The early settlers were of a religious turn of mind, and usually they had not been in a community long before they established a church.

When many of the small cabins built by the Scotch-Irish along the Catawba and its tributaries had been replaced by larger and more comfortable homes and when the fresh land was yielding plentiful crops, the thoughts of the people, now that living was somewhat easier, were turning toward education and the religion fostered by their covenant keeping ancestors. Their longings began to take form and were visualized in a church home in the wilderness to which they had come.

Was it incident or was it Providence that determined the location of their first church, "Old Goshen," as it was lovingly called by all Presbyterians of the county and many of other denominations whose beloved dead rest in its old cemetery?

As was often the case in those early days, a cemetery was started; then a church was built near the graves. The first body buried in what is now called the "Old Goshen Graveyard" was that of a lonely traveler passing through the country searching for a place to settle. He was encamped near the spring from which many, now living, drank water while in attendance upon all day preaching services in a church later built in a grove near-by. The stranger died and was buried on the hill opposite the place of his encampment.

A brush arbor was built. Here, at the forest shrine, by the stranger's lonely grave, the Scotch-Irish Presbyterians, a few of their A.R.P. friends, and some scattering English and Dutch who had affiliated with them, lifted their voices in prayer and songs of praise. The arbor was replaced by a little log church which was also used as a schoolhouse. The grave, and as time slipped by, the graves, the site of the brush arbor, and the little log church were enclosed at a later date within a stone wall now fast becoming a ruin.

The second church was built across a branch on the opposite hill near the spring. A flat rock on which generations have sat at lunch time is still plainly to be seen. This rock was the cornerstone of the second church, a larger log building. Later, in 1839, a frame building was erected, which is still standing and which was used as a preaching place until recent years.

Records of the establishment of Goshen prove it to be the oldest church in Gaston County and probably the first organized in North Carolina west of the Catawba River.

The Rev. J. K. Hall, present pastor of a new church formed from the old and taking its name, was brought up in Goshen. His father, the Rev. J. D. Hall, being pastor for many years, gives the following account of its organization: "The formal organization probably took place in 1764. In that year the Rev. Elihu Spencer and the Rev. Alexander

McWhorter were sent by the Synod of New York and Philadelphia to the 'back parts of North Carolina' for the express purpose of organizing churches and assisting them in settling their boundaries. In 1767 we find this record on the minutes of the Synod of New York and Philadelphia, 'Goshen, in the forks of the Catawba, petitions for someone to preach for them'." This shows a church existing in 1767.

The evidence, therefore, is almost conclusive that the formal establishment took place in 1764 when the commission was sent to the "back parts of North Carolina" for the express purpose of organizing churches. It is not known how long Goshen had been a preaching place prior to 1764.

During its early history Goshen depended for preaching on supplies sent out from the North. Missionary preachers came there from two to four times a year. Their comings were such great days in the lives of these God-fearing, liberty-loving people that from miles around they gathered. Some walked and the men carried guns on their shoulders as protection from Indians; others rode on horseback, the women riding behind and holding the babies. The distance traveled was often ten miles or more. They came together not only to hear the preaching of the gospel but also to obtain news from the outside world, especially from friends left behind in Pennsylvania.

Goshen did not have a regular pastor until several years after the Revolutionary War when the Rev. Humphrey Hunter, in 1795, was called for half his time. Some of the members signed the call and guaranteed him an annual salary of sixty-two pounds and ten shillings. The English pound was the current money of the colonies. James Kuykendall, a Dutchman from Holland, who had aligned himself with the Scotch-Irish and who in 1754 had settled at the mouth of Dutchman's Creek which was named for him, was one of the first elders of Goshen.

To "Old Goshen" came the pioneers, and through all the intervening years successive generations have come in summer's sun and winter's cold for inspiration and spiritual uplift, and have been so instilled with principals of faith and courage that they were enabled to go forth and join nobly in the conflicts of peace and war and to make great contribution to the development of Gaston County and North Carolina.

In 1767 we find this record on the minutes of the Synod of New York and Philadelphia, 'Goshen, in the forks of the Catawba, petitions for someone to preach for them'." This shows a church existing in 1767.

CHAPTER VIII

THE BOUNDARY LINE

An event which for years gave much concern to the pioneers of Gaston County was the North Carolina-South Carolina boundary dispute which lasted for almost a century. It began about 1720 when the purpose to erect a third province of Carolina, with the Savannah River for its northern boundary, began to assume definite shape. But the Lords Proprietors, not thinking the matter of much importance, sold their rights to the Crown without having fixed the limits of either colony. After the surrender of the charter it was thought best to put an end to the uncertainty. So in 1729-30 the newly appointed Governors of the two Carolinas, who were then in London, appeared before the Lords of the Boards of Trade and Plantations and made known to the Board that they had agreed upon a division line. The Governors, however, seemed not to have felt bound by their agreement, and the Lords of Trade withdrew their instructions to them and ordered that each province appoint a commission to run a certain line subject to the King's approval. Accordingly, an agreement was reached and the survey actually began on the first of May, 1735.

Every once in a while, the line was extended a few miles farther inland from the coast. In 1772, after making the required offset, which is a peculiar crook, so as to leave the Catawba Indians in South

Carolina, commissioners appointed by the Governors of the two provinces extended the line, in due west course, from the confluence of the South Fork and Catawba Rivers to Tryon Mountain. This was done according to the instruction of the Board of Trade sent out the year before.

The Legislature of North Carolina repudiated not only "the line of 1772" but also the authority by which it was run, contending that the parallel of thirty-five degrees of north latitude, having been the boundary by the agreement of 1735, could not be changed by a commission without the Legislature's consent. The Legislature maintained this position until 1813 when it agreed that "the line of 1772" should be recognized as part of the boundary.

The reason that the commissioners recommended this course and the Legislature finally agreed to it was that the observations of their own astronomer, President Caldwell of the University of North Carolina, showed that in running the line from the Pee Dee River to the Salisbury road it was not on the 35th parallel but some twelve miles to the south of it, and that "the line of 1772" was just about far enough north of the 35th parallel to rectify the error by allowing South Carolina to gain on the west of the Catawba substantially what she had lost on the east of it. The decision was that it was better to secure proffered confirmation of the line east of the Catawba by this restitution than to undo everything that had been done and go back to the 35th parallel for the line, though this was agreed to in the compromise of 1735.

The zigzag shape of the line as it runs from the southwest corner of Union County, North Carolina, to the Catawba River was necessary to throw the reservation of the Catawba Indians in the Province of South Carolina. The commissioners and surveyors were not "influenced by the close proximity of a still," as is sometimes claimed.

Along the borders of the disputed territory there was much wrangling over land grants. The South Carolina Governor would issue grants north of the 35th parallel and the North Carolina Governor for lands south of it. The result was the creation of a kind of sanctuary for criminals and vagabonds, who pretended that they belonged to either province as it served their purpose.

A marker, now deeply covered by the waters of the Duke Power development, stands at the confluence of the South Fork and Catawba Rivers opposite their juncture. The monument is of fine quality soapstone, ten inches square, highly polished, and neatly ornamented. It was exposed three feet above the sand bank in which it was imbedded, on the edge of an old ferry road abandoned long before it was covered by the Duke Power waters. On the well-preserved surface of the marker were carved numerous names and dates. But the inscription which aroused curiosity and seemed to hold the key to its history is on the south side and in the following words: "N. C.-S. C. Lat. 3500, J. M. Elford, by order of Gov. Geddes." Several questions come to mind. When was it erected? Why at this point and by what authority? If a cornerstone, why was the name of John Branch, Governor of North Carolina at that time, omitted?

After many inquiries, the following answer came from A. S. Salley, Jr., Secretary of the South Carolina Historical Commission: "It is true that a survey was made of the boundary line between the Carolinas on the mountain ridge between the end of the line of 1772 and the point of intersection of the 35th parallel with the Chattooga River. The work was completed Nov. 2, 1815, and ratified by the General Assembly of South Carolina, Dec. 15, 1815. David R. Williams was Governor at that time. Governor Geddes, during his administration from Dec., 1818 to Dec., 1820, had James M. Elford to make astronomical observations to ascertain the latitude and longitude at Ellicott's rock on the Chattooga River. He also took observations at other points.

"The marker in question, erected by Mr. Elford, as the inscription shows, was obviously placed while he was establishing the latitude of the boundary line. As it was done by order of Governor Geddes alone, Mr. Elford saw no reason why he should place thereon the name of the Governor of North Carolina.

"It was not set up to mark the boundary line officially as that had already been done by the representative of the two states in 1815."

The location of the water-covered marker is shown exactly by a map in possession of the Duke

Power Company. The people of York and Gaston Counties would feel grateful appreciation should this sentinel of more than a hundred years be raised from its watery bed and placed on the nearby sands. Then across its polished surface North Carolina and South Carolina could clasp hands in renewed affection, the quarrel of a hundred years lost and forgotten in mutual love and affection.

Note:

When Duke Power Company was contacted in 1997, officials could find no references to the marker in their archives. It is assumed that it remains beneath the waters of the Catawba and South Fork rivers.

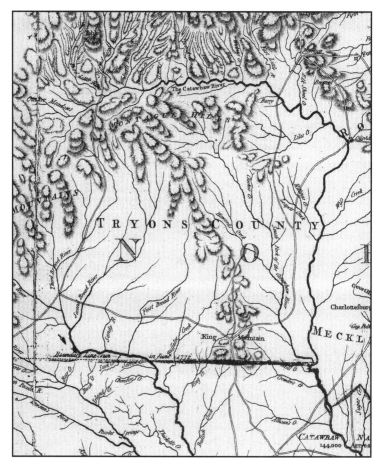

Detail of the 1775 Mouzon map.

ryon was a large county, forty-five miles from north to south and extending about eighty miles west from the Catawba River along what is now the South Carolina border. . . . In the heat of the Revolution, Tryon County, named for North Carolina's detested Governor William Tryon, disappeared. It had only lasted ten years.

CHAPTER IX

THE HOLDING OF COURTS MIDST THE RUMBLINGS OF WAR

The present Gaston County, then Tryon, during and long after the early Colonial period had past, was nothing more than an American frontier. The farms were mere patches surrounded by rail fences to protect the crops from roving cattle and wild animals. Roads, one-tracked and in winter knee-deep with mud, ran through virgin forests and connected the homes of the settlers, which were nearly always situated in out-of-the-way places by springs and along streams where water was plentiful for the families and their cattle and where pastures were rich and green. Communication was difficult, and sometimes for long periods the people had no news from the outside world. Gradually the roads were worked and kept in better condition. There were ferries and bridges across the streams, and, at an early date, a few Post Roads were made and mail routes established.

So the colonists were no longer entirely cut off, but learned something of what was taking place beyond their own communities.

The great question of taxation without representation was agitating the minds of the people. They resented the Stamp Act, which was a tax on tea and other commodities, because it was levied without their consent. They came to this country seeking the right to govern themselves, and they felt a deep sense of wrong when any attempt was made to deprive them of that privilege.

When, in 1775, Great Britain undertook the enforcement of her offensive laws, the liberty-loving people of the colonies, in one of the most dramatic episodes of history, seized their arms and, when necessary, left their homes and families and boldly asserted their right to liberty. They realized the conflict might be long and bitter, but they also knew that their freedom was threatened and that the result would mean that they would be either a free or a subordinate people—an empire was at stake and they arose heroically to meet the issue.

Tryon County, as well as other sections, began making preparations for war which now seemed inevitable.

Courts were held at the home of Christian Mauney during these troublous times. A strong sentiment was growing for separation from the Mother Country. This sentiment was intensified at the meetings of the Court, by which authority, bestowed by the Provincial Congress, a Safety Committee was elected by the people. One of the functions of the Safety Committees, which were organized in most counties, was to control the military activities of the counties and consequently of the colony.

The counties and their Committees of Safety were associated according to former judicial districts. So these districts became, as it were, the units of organization. Each county in a given district was required to raise at least one company and the larger counties two or three. The enlisted men were known as minutemen and were under militia officers. Those regularly enlisted were paid a bounty for enlisting and received pay while in active service. They were under strict military discipline, well organized, well trained, and ready at any time for active service. This accounts for the large number of militia captains killed at Ramseur's Mill. Hunter in his "Sketches of Western North Carolina" gives the number as seven.

While some were trained and received pay, it is well known that many men of what is now Gaston County were not enlisted, received no pay, and furnished their own food, obtained mostly from forest and stream. They were under no military authority; but learning of the necessity and actuated by patriotism, they left their plows in the furrows to join the forces at Ramseur's Mill, King's Mountain, and other places to fight valiantly for freedom.

Tryon was a large county, forty-five miles from north to south and extending about eighty miles west from the Catawba River along what is now the South Carolina border. It lost much territory to South Carolina when both states finally agreed to the boundary survey of 1772.

The county was set up from Mecklenburg in 1768, the Act becoming effective April 10, 1769. It was for several years without a permanent courthouse. The courts were held quarterly at some appointed place.

On Tuesday, December 14, 1773, a bill was passed by the Assembly in session at New Bern to appoint a Commission to build a courthouse, prison and stocks for the County of Tryon.

The Commission made the following report which was adopted at the July sessions of court, 1774:

North Carolina, Tryon County:

"We, the Commission appointed by the Act of Assembly for laying out and constituting and appointing the place whereon to erect and build the court house, prison and stocks of Tryon County, having maturely considered and deliberated on the same, are of the opinion that the place called the 'Cross Roads' on Christian Mauney's land, between the heads of Long Creek, Muddy Creek, and Beaverdam Creek in the county aforesaid, is most central and convenient for the purpose aforesaid for the inhabitants of this county: Therefore, agreeably to the directions of said Act, we have and by these presents do lay off, constitute, and appoint the said place as the most proper whereon to erect and build the court house, prison and stocks of the said county, as witness our hands and seals, the 26th day of July, A.D., 1774."

> CHARLES MCLEAN (*Seal*),
> WILLIAM MOORE (*Seal*),
> JOHN HILL (*Seal*),
> CHRISTOPHER CARPENTER (*Seal*).

It was then ordered that the next court be held at the home of Christian Mauney on the "Cross Roads" on his lands. This remained the site of the courthouse for nine years, and a room in his dwelling was used as a jail. The courthouse ordered by the assembly was never built; for, in the heat of the Revolution, Tryon County, named for North Carolina's detested Governor William Tryon, disappeared. It had lasted only ten years.

The Tryon Courts were styled the "County Court of Pleas and Quarter Sessions." In the court, deeds and wills were probated, estates settled, land entries recorded, guardians appointed, and orphans apprenticed. Roads were opened, overseers named, and many other matters pertaining to the interests of the people were attended to. There were a sheriff and clerk, a civil and criminal docket, grand and petit juries, and an "attorney for the Crown." County courts, wherever held, convened quarterly and continued without material change until the Constitution of 1868 was adopted.

One of the first orders of the Tryon Court was the granting of a license to Christian Mauney to run an ordinary in his home. Licenses were also granted to others. Roads were ordered laid out to the courthouse from various points in the county, and overseers for them were appointed.

In early pioneer days, the region near what was to be the site of the courthouse was one of the wildest of the county. Grass grew luxuriantly, providing pasturage for herds of fleet-footed deer and droves of buffalo. The woods were full of such wild beasts as preyed on domestic animals. Very early the settlers began setting a bounty on their scalps. In 1774, the year the courts began to be held at the home of Christian Mauney, forty-nine wolf scalps were paid for. Before that time the Red Man had left Indian Creek, the buffaloes had gone from their grazing places on Buffalo Mountain and the meadows of Buffalo Creek, and the beavers no longer built their dams on the creek that still bears their name.

The home of Christian Mauney remained the site of the courthouse for nine years, and a room in his dwelling was used as a jail.

In the court, deeds and wills were probated, estates settled, land entries recorded, guardians appointed, and orphans apprenticed. Roads were opened, overseers named, and many other matters pertaining to the interests of the people were attended to.

CHAPTER X

The Tryon Declaration of Independence was the third which predated that for all the colonies. The Mecklenburg came first on May 20, 1775. A month later, June 20, 1775, the people of Fayetteville, Cumberland County, in an officially signed document, declared their independence. This was followed by the Tryon Declaration on August 14, 1775. All three came several months before John Hancock put his famous signature to the Colonial document.

The Tryon Declaration was the outcome of the proceedings of the Safety Committee which met, according to adjournment, on August 14, 1775.

By authority of the Provincial Congress, the committee was elected by the freeholders of Tryon County on July 26, 1775. Those present at the August meeting were John Walker, who had already been chosen chairman, Thomas Beatty, David Jenkins, Jacob Forney, Thomas Espey, Valentine Mauney, James Coburn, Robert Alexander, Joseph H. Hardin, Benjamin Hardin, Frederick Hambright, James Logan, Andrew Hampton, John Morris, Charles McLean, John Robinson, George Black, William Graham, George Paris, John Beaman, Andrew Neel, James Baird, and David Whitesides. They took the necessary oath for their qualification. Andrew Neel was duly elected Clerk of the Committee.

A resolution was passed making Colonel Charles McLean deputy chairman to serve in the absence of Colonel Walker.

Another resolution was passed requiring each military company to elect three members to serve on the Safety Committee, each member to have a vote when a debate arose.

The Association or Declaration was embodied in the third resolution which reads as follows:

"Resolved, that this Association be signed by the inhabitants of Tryon County, (viz):

AN ASSOCIATION

"The unprecedented, barbarous and bloody actions committed by the British Troops on our American Brethren near Boston on the 19th of April and 20th of May last, together with the Hostile Operations and Traiterous Designs now carrying on by the Tools of Ministerial Vengeance and Despotism for the Subjugating all British America, suggest to us the painful necessity of having recourse to Arms for the preservation of those Rights and Liberties which the principles of our Constitution and the Laws of God, Nature and Nations have made it our duty to defend.

"We, therefore, the Subscribers, Freeholders and Inhabitants of Tryon County, do hereby faithfully unite ourselves under the most sacred ties of Religion, Honor and Love to our Country, firmly to resist force by force in defense of our Natural Freedom and Constitutional Rights against all invasions, and at the same time do solemnly engage to take up

Arms and Risque our lives and fortunes in maintaining the freedom of our Country, whenever the Wisdom and Council of the Continental Congress or our Provincial Convention shall declare it necessary, and this Engagement we will continue in and hold sacred 'till a Reconciliation shall take place between Great Britain and America on Constitutional principles which we most ardently desire. And we do firmly agree to hold all such persons Inimical to the liberties of America, who shall refuse to subscribe to this Association."

Signed by:

John Walker, Charles McLean, Andrew Neel, Thomas Beatty, James Coburn, Frederick Hambright, Andrew Hampton, Benjamin Hardin, George Paris, William Graham, Robt. Alexander, David Jenkins, Thomas Espey, James McAfee, William Thompson, Samuel Carpenter, Richard Woffer, Jacob Forney, David Whiteside, John Beaman, John Morris, Joseph Hardin, John Robison, Valentine Mauney, George Black, James Logan, Jas. Baird, Christian Carpenter, Abel Beatty, Joab Turner, Jonathan Price, Jas. Miller, John Dellinger, James McIntire, Peter Sides, William Whiteside, Geo. Dellinger, Jacob Mauney, Jr., John Wells, Jacob Costner, Robert Hulclip, James Buchanan, Moses Moore, Joseph Kuykendall, Adam Simms, Samuel Smith, Joseph Neel, Samuel Loftin, Peregrine Mackness.

The Tryon Declaration of Independence is commemorated by a stone marker on the site of the

Christian Mauney home used as a courthouse for nine years, until Tryon County disappeared.

After reaching this country these pioneers resided awhile in Pennsylvania and then came on to North Carolina, finally reaching the territory of the Beaver Dam, Indian, and Buffalo Creeks, where they felled the trees and built the cabins, the schoolhouse, and church. Along with tilling the virgin soil and causing the wilderness to blossom, they were making history but had no time to preserve it. So we can only catch glimpses of them as they went about the silent discharge of their private and public duties. They were strong men with brave spirits, willing to endure hardships and to face danger and even death, if necessary, rather than surrender their convictions.

True to their characteristics, many of this section later joined others from more distant parts of the county in signing the Tryon Declaration.

The Tryon Declaration of Independence was the third which predated that for all the colonies. The Mecklenburg came first on May 20, 1775. A month later, June 20, 1775, the people of Fayetteville . . . declared their independence. This was followed by the Tryon Declaration on August 14, 1775.

CHAPTER XI

After Tryon County disappeared in 1779, Lincoln and Rutherford took its place. Many of the men continued in military service, fighting Cherokee Indians and putting down Tory uprisings on the South Carolina border. They volunteered to join military units and went with them where needed. This continued until 1780 when a regiment of Lincoln County men was formed with William Graham, Colonel, Frederick Hambright, Lieutenant Colonel, and William Chronicle, Major. A large number of those composing this regiment lived in lower Lincoln, later Gaston County. Not counting the reserves under Colonel James Johnston, there were about sixty in all. Twenty of them were devoted friends and neighbors of Major Chronicle and were known as the "South Fork boys." Inspired by the zeal and patriotism of their leader, they were ever ready to stand or fall by his side.

When it was learned that Ferguson, with his British and Tories, was preparing for battle and that the men from over the mountains were gathering in pursuit of him, several detachments joined the mountaineers on their march to the Cowpens, their place of rendezvous. Major William Chronicle, with his twenty "South Fork boys," joined them at Probit's Place on Broad River and marched with them to the Cowpens. (This information was preserved by Robert Henry, one of the "Fork boys," who lived to a great old age in Buncombe County.) On October 2nd, two hundred seventy South Carolinians of Sumter's command crossed the Catawba at the Tuckaseege ford and encamped in the fork of that stream. Here they were joined by Colonel Graham and Lieutenant Colonel Hambright with a small force of about forty men. Major Chronicle and his "South Fork boys" had gone on ahead. Colonel Williams and his followers marched with the regular South Carolina and Lincoln County men.

Ferguson, knowing that strong forces were pursuing him, was marching toward Charlotte; but his infatuation for military glory caused him to delay when he could easily have reached the camp of Cornwallis. His hope of undying fame was changed to defeat, disaster, and death.

The Whig forces met at the Cowpens and pursued Ferguson, coming up with him at King's Mountain where that memorable battle was fought which broke the Tory power and turned the tide of the Revolution.

The following is a partial roll call and record of Gaston County men who had part in this battle or other engagements of the Revolution which helped mould the feeble colonies into a powerful nation:

MAJOR WILLIAM CHRONICLE

Major William Chronicle was one of the greatest heroes of that grand romance of history, the battle of King's Mountain, the turning point in our conflict for freedom.

He was born about the year 1755 and was reared in what is now the town of Belmont. The old family home was known as the "Mansion House" and stood just across the street from the Chronicle Mill named in honor of his memory.

His mother first married a Mr. McKee in Pennsylvania. With him she moved to North Carolina and settled near the South Fork River in what was then Anson, now Gaston County. By this marriage she had one son, James McKee, a soldier of the Revolution and ancestor of the several families of that name in this vicinity. The remains of this half-brother of Major Chronicle rest in New Hope Cemetery.

After McKee's death his widow married William Chronicle and changed her place of residence to the "Mansion House." His will, written by his own hand in the year 1785, shows him to have been a God-fearing man, a man of considerable learning for his day and time, and possessed of lands, negroes, and stock. He owned all the land on which Belmont now stands, having purchased it from William Barnett, who obtained it by patent from the King. Major Chronicle was a young man of twenty-five and unmarried at the time of his death, so his father's property went mostly to the children of his sister, Sarah Chronicle Scott.

The testimony of all who knew Major Chronicle represented him to be a ceaseless, untiring defender of liberty, exerting an effective influence in spreading the doctrine of independence throughout the lower portion of old Lincoln County. Colonel

Graham described him as being "a young man of great promise—the idol of his friends and soldiers." His pleasing personality won for him the high regard of people generally, and helped him greatly in making successful his appeals to their patriotism.

His first military service was performed in December, 1775. He was at the head of a company in the Snow campaign and in 1779 marched to Georgia and afterwards to the relief of Charleston. After the battle of Ramseur's Mill, he was engaged for a while in chasing Tories out of the country. Early in the fall of 1780 a regiment was formed in Lincoln County, of which Gaston was then a part. William Graham was made Colonel; Frederick Hambright, Lieutenant Colonel; and William Chronicle, Major. This regiment, including Major Chronicle and his twenty "South Fork boys," met Campbell, Shelby, Cleveland, Sevier, and others at or near the Cowpens and joined in the pursuit of Ferguson, coming up with him at King's Mountain and taking part in the battle. If Draper is correct, it was upon information furnished by Major Chronicle and his scout, Gilmer, that the battle was planned. The following is taken from Draper's "King's Mountain and its Heroes":

"The other officers decided it was necessary to have a scout to keep up with the movements of Ferguson. Major Chronicle selected Enoch Gilmer of the South Fork. It was objected that Gilmer was not acquainted with the country. Chronicle replied that Gilmer could acquire information better than those who knew the region more thoroughly, and could readily assume any character that occasion might require.

"He could laugh or cry in the same breath, and act the part of a lunatic so well that those best acquainted with him could readily believe him deranged. It was then agreed that Gilmer should go."

When the mountaineers had advanced to within a short distance of Ferguson's camp, Sevier's men called at the house of a Loyalist and sought information. The Loyalist would only reply that "Ferguson is not far away." As they departed, a girl followed the riflemen out of the building and inquired, "How many are there of you?" "Enough," was the reply, "to whip Ferguson if we can find him." "He is on that mountain," said she, pointing to the eminence not far distant. After traveling on a little way the officers in front saw the horse of Gilmer fastened to a gate. On going into the house they found Gilmer sitting at a table eating. "We have got you!" exclaimed Colonel Campbell. "I am a true King's man," replied Gilmer. Campbell threw a lasso over his head and declared he meant to hang him. Chronicle interceded and begged that he should not be hanged there, for his ghost would haunt the women. When they got out of sight of the house, he was released and gave the intelligence he had gained. He said that on reaching the house he declared himself to be a Loyalist and was anxious to find the location of Ferguson's camp, because he wished to join him. Finding the two women of the house warmly attached to the King's cause, he could not repress his sympathetic joy. He so gained the good will of the women that they told the location of the camp and said that they had carried Ferguson some chickens that very morning.

They said Ferguson was posted on a ridge between two branches where some deer hunters had had a camp the previous fall. Major Chronicle and Captain Mattocks stated that the camp had been theirs and that they well knew the ground on which Ferguson had taken his post, a spur of King's Mountain.

Based upon the information gained from Gilmer, the officers, after a short consultation, agreed upon a plan of attack.

Colonel William Graham, who was at the head of the Lincoln men, presumably at this point had a message from home saying that his wife was seriously ill and that his presence was demanded at the earliest possible moment. Leave of absence was granted him. Campbell then said to Major Chronicle, "You must take Graham's place." Lieutenant Colonel Hambright added that it was his desire also, since Chronicle best knew the ground. So it was satisfactorily arranged and Chronicle, as acting Colonel of the Lincoln regiment, took the lead. He called first upon the boys of his home section, saying, "Come on, my South Fork boys; never let it be said that a Fork boy ran."

This appeal was not given in vain. Every man was nerved for the conquest. Onward the brave soldiers steadily marched. They were led up the northeast end of the mountain. As they reached the base of the ridge, Chronicle, a little in advance of his men, raised his military hat, crying out, "Face to the hill!" He had scarcely uttered his command when a ball struck him in the breast, and he fell mortally wounded.

William Caldwell, a neighbor, who was also in the battle, brought home Major Chronicle's horse and put it in his father's stable, saddled as it was at the battle. Next morning when his father found it, he knew his son was dead. His sword and spurs passed into the hands of his half-brother, James McKee, and were taken by one of his sons to Tennessee.

While unmarried, Major Chronicle's life was not without romance. He was to have married Margaret Alexander, a daughter of Robert Alexander and Mary Jack who lived at Woodlawn, now Mt. Holly. Mary Jack Alexander was a sister of Captain James Jack, who carried the Mecklenburg Declaration of Independence to Philadelphia. When Major Chronicle was killed, he had on his finger a ring given him by Miss Alexander. About eight years after the death of Major Chronicle, Margaret Alexander married Judge Samuel Lowry. Their son, Robert B. Lowry, married Ann Sloan of Mecklenburg.

The following is the will of William Chronicle, father of Major William Chronicle, written in 1785, probated in 1786:

"In the name of God, amen. I, William Chronicle of the County of Lincoln, and State of North Carolina, being in good health and of sound mind and memory, and calling to mind that it is appointed for all men to die and knowing the frailty of man; do make and ordain this to be my last will and testament, hereby I, making all wills hereto before made by me void and do alone order and make this to be my last will in manner and form following: That is to say, Imprimus! I recommend my soul to God who gave it and my body I request may receive a decent burial agreeable to the pleasure of my Executors hereafter named.

"In expectation of a joyful resurrection at the great and awful day through the merits of our blessed Lord and Savior Jesus Christ and for what worldly goods it has pleased God to bestow upon me, I request and order to be divided in the following manner: (viz.) Item. I give and bequeath unto my well beloved wife, Dinah Chronicle, one feather bed and furniture to her and her heirs forever, also I lend my said wife all and singular the negroes I die possessed of and the Mansion House and the land I live on for and during her natural life and then to be distributed as hereafter directed, further, I order that my said wife have two horses and plows and gears sufficient to tend the plantation and further all other necessary tools for and during her said life and further, I desire that all my just debts be paid and that my Executors see that my will be particularly executed and after the decease of my said wife I request that William Scott, my grandson, and son of my daughter, Sarah Scott, have three hundred acres of the land I live on with the Mansion House and half of the cleared ground to him and his heirs forever.

"Item. I give and bequeath unto my grandson, John Scott, brother of above, one hundred and twenty acres, part of the above tract, and joining Samuel Caldwell's line on the main road to him and his heirs forever.

"Item. I desire that my well beloved friend, Edward Hunter, for the many services already done and to do have one horse or the value thereof out of my estate immediately after my death, after this my will is proved: which I allow to be twenty-five pounds and further I order that my executors sell and dispose of all and singular of my estate, real and personal, that is not already given or lent, and the money arising therefrom. After my debts are paid, be immediately lent out on interest until my grandchildren, the sons and daughters of my daughter, Sarah Scott, shall arrive at the age of twenty-one years and then to be equally divided amongst them to be theirs and their heirs' property forever. And after the death of my beloved wife, Dinah, I order that all and singular of the estate lent to her be equally divided as above amongst my said grandchildren, the children of my said daughter, Sarah Scott, and lastly I nominate and appoint my beloved wife, Dinah Chronicle, George Ewing and James Henderson executors of this my last will and testament in witness whereof I have hereunto set my hand and seal, this the 3rd day of August in the year of our Lord, Christ. One thousand seven hundred and eighty-five."

Signed, Sealed, Published and Declared
In presence of
EDWARD HUNTER—*Just*.
JUDITH SCOTT HUNTER
POLINA HUNTER

LIEUTENANT COLONEL FREDERICK HAMBRIGHT

A short sketch of Lieutenant Colonel Hambright as one of the early German pioneers has already been given. True to his pioneering spirit and German thriftiness he had obtained by patent several tracts of land in what is now Gaston County. At the time of the Revolutionary War and the battle of King's Mountain, he was living on land granted him in May, 1769, in the fork of Long Creek and a branch then known as Still House Branch near Dallas. His first wife, Sarah Hardin, died during the Revolution. She lies in a neglected, unmarked grave on the place. Shortly before the battle, he had purchased land on King's Creek near the battleground, and had built a cabin preparatory to moving his family there.

Lieutenant Colonel Hambright was a brave soldier and at that time was the highest ranking officer living in what is now Gaston County.

As early as 1771, Frederick Hambright, then a captain, went against the Cherokees, for which services he and his men were paid by the state.

He, as a member of the Committee of Safety for Tryon County, had much to do with directing military activities just prior to and during the early part of the Revolution. In 1775, he was appointed major of the militia or minutemen. In August of the same year he was elected to the Provincial Congress. At a meeting of the Tryon Safety Committee on September 14, 1775, it was agreed to make application to the Council of Safety of Charles Town for purchases of gunpowder, lead, and flints, because lives on the frontier were much exposed to the insults of the savages. In June, 1776, he served on the frontier. In the fall of the same year he was with General Rutherford in the Cherokee campaign. Late in 1779, he went to the relief of Charleston. He served in Lillington's brigade and returned before the surrender of that place.

It is known by extracts found in "Colonial Records of North Carolina" that Frederick Hambright was called often from his home to positions of honor and trust where wise council was needed, even before he began his military career which terminated in distinguished service at King's Mountain.

He served under Colonel McDowell near Broad River.

Early in the fall of 1780 a regiment was raised in Lincoln County with William Graham, Colonel; Frederick Hambright, Lieutenant Colonel; and William Chronicle, Major.

A short time before the battle of King's Mountain, Governor Nash had granted Colonel Williams of South Carolina the privilege of organizing a corps of mounted men within the Northern Province. About 70 men were enlisted under this authority. On the 2nd of October, 1780, they crossed the

Catawba at Tuckaseege ford. Here between the Catawba and the South Fork he found Sumter's command under Colonels Hill and Lacy. This party, for its own safety, had retired from South Carolina.

That same day the South Carolinians were also joined by Colonel William Graham and Lieutenant Colonel Hambright with a small party of perhaps 40 men, mostly from the lower part of the present Gaston County. Major Chronicle with 20 men from the South Fork of the Catawba had already joined the men from over the mountains at what was called Probit's Place on Broad River. The number of Chronicle's men was preserved by Robert Henry, one of the party.

If the number of Hambright's and Chronicle's men together was 60, as is generally conceded, and there is a definite knowledge that Chronicle's was 20, then Graham and Hambright had 40 when they joined the South Carolinians. Because of a dispute with Colonel Williams who desired entire control of the forces, at the suggestion of Colonel Hill of Sumter's command it was proposed that the troops should be arranged in three divisions: the South Carolinians proper, Graham and Hambright's party, and the followers of Williams. To this Williams reluctantly agreed, and the march to join the mountain men began. It led them through the upper part of the present Gaston County. Crossing the upper fork of Dutchman's Creek, they continued until they finally reached the Cowpens on October the 6th. Soon after their arrival they were joined by the men from over the mountains, to which force

Major Chronicle and his twenty "South Fork boys" had already attached themselves.

Marching from the Cowpens, they came upon Ferguson at King's Mountain and the battle resulted. At a council of the Whig officers Lieutenant Colonel Hambright displayed his real nobility of character when, though being of highest rank, he agreed that Major Chronicle, because of peculiar fitness, should lead the Lincoln men. Colonel Graham had been excused because of illness in his family. Hambright, early in the action, was severely wounded in the thigh. In spite of the protests of his soldiers, he retained his saddle and fought on until the battle was over. When finally he alighted from his horse, the blood was running over the boot on the foot of his wounded leg. He was conveyed to the cabin previously built by him on King's Creek near the field of action, and here he was carefully nursed. Finally, he partly regained his strength, although he limped from the effects of the wound for the balance of his life.

His services at King's Mountain were so outstanding that when the General Assembly met at Halifax early in 1781, he and others were publicly commended, on behalf of their country, for their heroism and patriotism. Then a resolution was read that an elegantly mounted sword be presented to him.

After the war Frederick Hambright continued in public service. He and Nicholas Friday, who settled near High Shoals, were members of a commission to select the site of Lincoln County Court House and other public buildings, to purchase land on which to erect said buildings, and also to give contract to workers. This was done in 1782.

Soon after the battle, he sold his farm on Long Creek and moved to the King's Creek neighborhood. Here with his second wife, Mary Dover, he lived until March 9, 1817, dying in the 90th year of his age, and was buried in the cemetery of Shiloh Presbyterian Church of which he had been an elder for many years. A plain slab marks his grave. He left a large family of children and has many descendants in Gaston, Lincoln, and Cleveland Counties. One son, John, a captain, also fought at King's Mountain. Another son, his namesake, Frederick, afterward known as Major Frederick Hambright, was a boy of twelve at the time of the battle. He it was who preserved a long string of small beads worn by "Virginia Sal" when she was killed early in the action. She lay all night, unburied, on the mountain side.

Lieutenant Colonel Hambright was a man of sterling qualities, brave in battle, patient in suffering, rugged and manly.

ISAAC HOLLAND, SR.

Isaac Holland was born May 12, 1745. The family came to this country from England. The place of landing and date of arrival are not known with certainty, nor the time of their coming to Gaston County. Perhaps they were too badly frightened to remember dates as the following "fish story" would indicate: The ship on which they came from England began to leak. Every means known to the crew for stopping the hole or keeping the water pumped out was tried to no avail. When all hope of saving the vessel had been given up, the leak suddenly stopped and a safe landing was made. Upon examination it was found that a fish had run up into the hole and was caught by its fins, thus stopping the leak. So the vessel was saved.

Isaac Holland, upon first coming to Gaston, settled on the south side of Catawba Creek near the present limits of Gastonia where he had large tracts of land, now in possession of a branch of the Lineberger family, a member of which married a Holland. The old home site was below Mrs. Will Lineberger's and now belongs to Eli P. Lineberger, a great-great grandson of Isaac Holland, Sr.

Isaac Holland, Sr., was a private in the Revolution and fought at King's Mountain. Tradition says he walked home the night following the battle, notwithstanding his strenuous exertions in the fight.

In 1770 he married Hannah Liggit or Legett, a young widow whose maiden name was Wiley. She was born October 29, 1747, and died June 2, 1818. The names of the following children of Isaac Holland, Sr., were taken from the family records: Mary, Margaret, Jean, Isaac, Oliver, James, and Hannah.

Isaac Holland, Sr., died October 10, 1810, and is buried by the side of his wife in the old part of Olney Cemetery near Gastonia.

The above information was furnished by Mrs. Clara Holland Falls, Gastonia, and Mrs. Nellie

Roseman Eddleman, Gastonia, both descendants of Isaac Holland, Sr.

DR. WILLIAM MCLEAN

Dr. William McLean was the son of Alexander and Elizabeth Ratchford McLean. He was born in Rowan County, North Carolina, on Sunday, the 2nd day of April, 1757. He had three sisters, Margaret, Agnes, and Jean, who were born while the family lived in Pennsylvania where it first resided after reaching this country from the North of Ireland. Two of these died of smallpox before the father, mother, and other child removed to North Carolina where the oldest son, John, was born. Soon after the birth of William, another move was made to a tract of land near the junction of the South Fork and Catawba Rivers, where three more brothers of Dr. McLean were born. Their names were Alexander, George, and Thomas.

The early life of William was spent on his father's farm where he shared the many tasks which usually fell to the lot of the average farm boy. In his mind there was a constantly growing desire for education, which later developed him as a man of liberal culture. This is shown by the large number of well-chosen books he possessed. These were mostly works on medicine, science, religion, general literature, and poetry.

He went to the neighborhood schools and, being unusually bright in his books, advanced rapidly. His instructor during the last three months of his rural school life, a Mr. Blythe, a man of vision who noticed in his pupil more than ordinary capacity, advised him to go to Queen's Museum in Charlotte. The advice was taken and he became a Queen's Museum pupil along with many of the leading patriots of the Revolution. To the president of that institution, Rev. Alexander McWhorter, a distinguished Presbyterian preacher, goes the credit of instilling in his pupils those principles of civil and religious liberty which gave them excellency as military leaders.

William McLean remained in this institution about two years, during which time he made up his mind to become a physician. Getting together all the medical books he could procure, he took them home and devoted himself dutifully to their study. In the earlier stages of his preparation, he was offered the position of "Surgeon's Mate" in the Continental army by Dr. Joseph Blythe. He accepted this position. They both marched with the army to James Island near Charleston. At Stono, in June, 1779, a severe but indecisive battle had been fought between a detachment of General Lincoln's army and the British. At the time of Dr. McLean's arrival in the vicinity, many soldiers were sick with camp fever or were in the army hospital suffering from the wounds of battle. Some of these men were from Dr. McLean's own community, and he was personally acquainted with them. Most of them, under his ministrations, were soon restored to health and ready to re-enter the service of their country.

The Tories in upper South Carolina, during the summer and fall of 1780, were both numerous and troublesome. Dr. McLean was constantly with the southern army at this time, watching the movements of Ferguson in the Tory settlements just prior to his defeat and death at King's Mountain. After this battle many a brave hero was relieved of pain, comforted, and cheered by the tender ministrations of Dr. McLean. He kept up the good work by accompanying some of the wounded to a Charlotte hospital where he continued to look after them. He was with General Green's army near Camden. Here and at other military encampments, he faithfully discharged the duties of "Surgeon's Mate" until the close of the war. Afterwards, he completed his medical education at the University of Pennsylvania and received his diploma in 1787. He came home and settled on a farm near the family estate on the banks of the South Fork and soon built up an extensive practice. This farm has long been owned and occupied by a descendant and namesake, William or "Button" McLean, as he is familiarly known, who is a son of Robert McLean. When the house now standing was built, a brick from the old house, bearing the date 1794, was placed in the chimney of the new. The office used by Dr. McLean is still standing in Mr. William McLean's yard. His watch, a solid gold key winder, costing $500, is in possession of Erwin, son of William McLean, and a great grandson of Dr. William McLean.

After the Revolution had ended, doubt and distrust prevailed everywhere. In the rank and file of the American army as well as in all branches of civil life, the finances of the nation were exhausted. The situation ahead was one to daunt even the patriot, Washington. In order to protect themselves and their beloved country from a possible impending danger, to perpetuate the friendships they had formed, to aid each other in the future by substantial acts of beneficence, and to promote and cherish that union and honor between the states so vitally necessary for the preservation of the new government, the officers of the American army united themselves, before their final disbandment, into a "Society of Friends," styled the Cincinnati, to endure as long as they endured or any of their male posterity or in failure there, a descendant of a collateral branch "who may be judged worthy to become its supporter." Dr. McLean was one of the charter members of the North Carolina branch of this Society organized at Hillsboro, October 23, 1783. Robert Adams of Gastonia was his representative in 1825. P. W. Garland, also of Gastonia, representing an entire branch, is also a member.

On June 19, 1792, Dr. McLean married Mary, third daughter of Major John Davidson, a signer of the Mecklenburg Declaration of Independence. By this marriage he had ten children, one of whom, Dr. John McLean, was the progenitor of most of the McLean family still living in the South Point and other sections of Gaston County.

Dr. McLean was elected State Senator in 1814. During the summer of that same year, through his efforts, a day was set apart and the human bones, which were gruesome reminders of the struggle at

King's Mountain and which had been dragged by wolves from their shallow graves, were gathered together and reinterred. The old monument of dark slate rock, the first to be placed there, was erected at the expense of Dr. McLean. In celebration of its erection on July 4, 1814, he delivered a beautiful and scholarly address of great historical value. It is to be regretted that it has not been preserved in full. Part was published in the *Gastonia Gazette* of Saturday, August 21, 1880. The manuscript was furnished by the late Mrs. Charles Adams, a granddaughter of Dr. McLean.

When North Carolina ceded to the Federal government the lands now embraced in the State of Tennessee, certain portions were reserved and given to North Carolina soldiers who had distinguished themselves during the Revolution. Dr. McLean was one of the beneficiaries, having received a tract of this land. A copy of the grant states that the land was on Red River in Tennessee and was given to Dr. McLean by the State of North Carolina, and consisted of two thousand five hundred sixty acres. He made a trip there to have the land surveyed. While on the journey, he wrote a very interesting letter to his wife describing incidents along the way.

Dr. McLean is described as being an unusually handsome man—six feet tall, straight as an arrow, and of the most polished manners.

After a life of great usefulness, he died on the 25th of October, 1828, in the 72nd year of his age. His wife survived her husband many years. The lives of both were dignified by the religion which they professed. They were members of Bethel Presbyterian Church, York County, S. C., and their bodies repose with many other illustrious dead in its historic cemetery.

CAPTAIN SAMUEL MARTIN

Captain Samuel Martin was a man in whose breast fiercely burned the fires of patriotism and who deserves more than passing notice because of his long and loyal service to his country in its conflict for freedom.

His father, Hugh Martin, was born in Tyrone County, Ireland, in 1700. He married Jane Hunter in 1731. Soon after his marriage he emigrated to America and settled in Hunterdon County, New Jersey, where he reared a large family of children. Samuel, born in 1732, was probably the oldest. He came to Gaston County sometime before the Revolution and settled on land granted him by the King. The land is now in possession of the Ratchfords, and was the home place of the late R. A. Ratchford. One of his six living sons, Mr. Duff Ratchford, at the present time occupies the new house built by his father before his death. The Martin land came down to them through direct descent from Samuel Martin. The old Martin home is still standing about one hundred yards away, in a good state of preservation. The house conforms somewhat to the Dutch type of architecture, with its two stories, its room on one end of the porch, and its great eight-foot fireplace in which the pot hooks still hang. The location is rugged and hilly. It is built near a spring, and surrounding cedars, a few moss roses, and crepe myrtles remain to attest former loveliness. The location is about midway between the New Hope and Union sections on Catawba Creek and about one and one-half miles from the South Carolina line. Samuel Martin's children, of whom there were several, settled on parts of the original farm near the parental home. In June, 1776, Samuel Martin entered military service as a private in Captain Robert Alexander's company, Colonel Graham's regiment, and marched across the Blue Ridge against the Cherokees. In June, 1777, he joined Captain William Chronicle's command and went to the relief of Ninety-Six in South Carolina. He then returned to North Carolina. About the first of November, 1779, his company was ordered to Charlotte where General Rutherford conferred on him a special commission of captain. With his special command and other forces from Charlotte, he marched to the relief of Charleston. Finding that place completely invested by the British army, he returned to North Carolina about June 1, 1780, with Colonel Graham's regiment.

On the night of his arrival home, he was told that the Tories had gathered in strong force at Ramseur's Mill. Immediately he raised a small company and joined other patriots, under General Rutherford, and encamped at Colonel Dickson's plantation, three miles northwest of Tuckaseege ford. On the morning of the 20th of June, 1780, they marched to Ramseur's Mill, but found the battle over and the Tories defeated and routed by Colonel Locke. After the battle, Martin was sent to capture Colonel

Moore, the Tory leader, but he had fled with about 30 of his followers to Camden, South Carolina, to join Cornwallis. Captain Martin spent the following two or three months chasing Tories, mainly in South Carolina. During the latter part of August and the entire month of September he was rarely at home, and then for only a couple of days at a time.

About the last week in September he marched with his company, under Colonel Graham, to the Cowpens. There, uniting with Colonels Campbell, Shelby, Sevier, Cleveland and others, he went with them to King's Mountain. In this battle Captain Martin was in the thickest of the fight and lost six of his company. After the battle he did scouting duties wherever his services were needed.

On May 13, 1833, he made application for a pension, which was allowed.

He died November 26, 1836, aged 104 years, and is buried beside his wife, Margaret McReady Martin, in the old Goshen Cemetery. His grave is marked by a stone erected by a grandson, Rev. W. Martin, in 1857, on which is the following inscription: "Capt. of a troop in the Revolution. He did good service at King's Mountain."

Many descendants are scattered over the county. One brother, Alexander Martin, who settled in Guilford County, served two terms as governor of North Carolina. Samuel Martin was a member of the Associate Reformed Church, a man outstanding for honor, integrity, and bravery.

The above data was secured mainly from family records gathered and preserved by the late Mrs.

M. A. Rhyne, of near Gastonia. Mrs. Rhyne was a direct descendant of Captain Martin. Additional facts were gathered from Hunter's "Sketches of Western North Carolina" and other sources.

CAPTAIN JOHN MATTOCKS

The Mattockses were a family that came into the county before the Revolution. It is not known from where they came. There were three brothers, John, Charles, and Ned, and two sisters, Sallie and Barbara. As a family they were distinguished for their prowess and great physical strength. The late A. J. Smith, noted for his knowledge of local history, told the following story of the Mattockses: "One day a great bully from another state approached the house, which was enclosed by a rail fence. He was talking in a very domineering manner, when one of the sisters picked him up by the seat of his pants and set him over the fence. He left and was heard of no more." This took place, according to Mr. Smith, on what was later the Hall farm near Belmont, where they lived. The home site may still be seen.

John and Charles were brave Whigs, always ready to serve their country, but Ned was a Tory. All three were at the battle of King's Mountain. Captain John Mattocks was killed early in the action. Ned, the Tory brother, was severely wounded. The next day, Charles, fearing his brother would be hanged, interceded for him, took him home, and carefully nursed him until he recovered from his wound and his Toryism.

The Mattockses likely stayed in the county for a few years after the war. In Vol. 17, p. 22, Colonial Records, it is stated that army pay for John Mattocks was collected. In 1784 a recommendation was made to the North Carolina General Assembly by Lincoln County in favor of Rachel Mattocks. It was endorsed by the speaker of each house and returned.

A few years after the war, the entire surviving family moved to Georgia. Major William Chronicle, Captain John Mattocks, who was his dear friend and companion on many hunts, William Rabb, and John Boyd, all "South Fork boys," lie buried in a common grave at the foot of the spur of the mountain on which they fell.

JOSEPH DICKSON

Joseph Dickson was a Scotch-Irishman, born about 1745. He came to North Carolina before the Revolution. After moving about a bit, he settled on the west side of the Catawba River, full three miles northwest of Tuckaseege ford. Here with his wife, Margaret McEwen, of Scotch family, he developed one of the finest plantations in lower Lincoln, now Gaston County. Still standing in a beautiful grove is the brick part of the old home and one brick outbuilding. A bold spring near by was the source of the water supply. An old road, still plainly visible, led to the house.

It was on this plantation that General Rutherford and his men camped for the night on June 19, 1780, after crossing the Catawba on their way to Ramseur's Mill to take part in the battle against

the Tories gathered there. Because of a misunder-
standing, they failed to reach their destination until
the battle was over.

Besides his farming interests Joseph Dickson took
an active part in civil, military, and religious affairs.
During the Revolutionary period he was considered
one of the county's most prominent men. When
the first census was taken in 1790, he was one of
its largest slave holders. In 1781 he was chosen
Clerk of the Court. Beginning in 1788, he served
in the State Senate for seven years and in Congress
for one term from 1797 to 1801.

He was made a captain in 1779. In June, 1780,
he joined the forces of General Rutherford and
helped rid the county of Tories. After the death
of Major Chronicle at King's Mountain, he took his
place as major and assisted in leading the Lincoln
men up the mountain. In 1781 he was made
colonel, and later he was made general of militia
after opposing the invasion of North Carolina by
Cornwallis.

He was a member of old Goshen Church and
signed the call for its first regular pastor.

Later, he moved to Tennessee and died there on
April 14, 1825, and was buried with military and
Masonic honors.

Many people have since owned the old plantation. It is now the property of the children of Ural
Johnston.

ROBERT ALEXANDER

About 1760 Robert Alexander came to North
Carolina from Pennsylvania. While it is supposed

that he was of the Mecklenburg Alexanders, nothing is positively known of his ancestry or where
he first settled after arrival. If it were in Mecklenburg, he later crossed over the Catawba and located
on a farm about a mile northwest of Tuckaseege
ford where Mt. Holly now stands. His residence was
called Woodlawn. From that fact the town was
given the name of Woodlawn by which it was
known for a number of years. The house, which
was a general stopping place for travelers, was
painted red; hence it was also widely known as the
"red house place."

His was a vision so broad that it included not
only home and farm but also county and state, and
guided him to many duties both civil and military. He commanded a company in the Cherokee
expedition and was a captain in the Revolution.
Dr. Hunter, in his "Sketches of Western North
Carolina," mentions several individual soldiers who
were in his company. He attended the New Bern
Convention in August of 1774 and the Hillsboro
Convention of 1775.

He was one of the freeholders of Tryon County
who met at the courthouse of said county on July
26, 1775, for the purpose of selecting a safety committee to direct the military affairs and to look after
the welfare of the people of the county generally. He
was later a member of the committee which held
one of its first meetings on August 14, 1775, and
drew up the resolutions of the Tryon Association
or Declaration of Independence which he, with
many others, signed.

His family life is interesting. His first wife was Mary Jack, third daughter of Captain Patrick Jack and the sister of Captain James Jack, who carried the Mecklenburg Declaration of Independence to Philadelphia. The eldest daughter, Margaret, by this marriage, was the betrothed of Major William Chronicle when he fell at King's Mountain. After having mourned for her gallant lover for eight years, she married Judge Samuel Lowry, by whom she had several children.

Dr. J. C. Rudisill married Amanda, the youngest daughter of Robert Alexander by a second wife. He practiced medicine throughout the section for many years. He then moved to Lincolnton and sold part of the Alexander home place to A. P. Rhyne who built on it the first cotton mill of the town and gave it the name of Mt. Holly because of the number of beautiful holly trees growing there.

Robert Alexander was elected to the Legislature consecutively from 1781 to 1787, and in addition performed many minor but important trusts for the county.

As a prominent member of Goshen Church he was one of the number to present the call to Rev. Humphrey Hunter.

After a useful life he died in 1813, aged about 70 years, and is buried somewhere in Goshen Cemetery.

COLONEL JAMES JOHNSTON

Henry Johnston of Scotch descent was the first of the Johnston family to settle in the present Gaston County. He located on the west bank of the Catawba River with his wife who died young, leaving two children. They were James, the subject of this sketch, and Mary who married Moses Scott and settled near Goshen Church. Moses Scott and Mary Johnston had three children, James J., William, and Abram Scott. William married Sarah Chronicle, only sister of Major William Chronicle.

James Johnston was born about 1742 and is said to have inherited some of the traits for which the family was noted in Scotland; such as, being heady, strong-minded, proud, and rebellious.

He occupied an enviable position among his friends and neighbors. With Colonel Charles McLean, he represented Tryon County in the Provincial Congress which met at Halifax on April 4, 1776. This congress was one of the most important ever held in the state. The delegates were empowered to concur with the delegates from other colonies in declaring independence.

Colonel Johnston's first military service was in the Snow campaign of '76. With his companions he had a great deal of war experience fighting the Cherokee Indians and helping to put down Tory uprisings in upper South Carolina. On one of these expeditions he nearly lost his life in a personal encounter with Patrick Moore, a Tory officer. He captured the Tory and was bearing him to the Whig lines near by, when he saw several British troopers approaching. He attempted to shoot them, but his musket missed fire. The prisoner escaped, and Johnston saved himself by hiding in a thicket.

Colonel Johnston was present at Ramseur's Mill, but participated only in the closing duties of that engagement because he had been sent by Colonel Locke, then encamped near the scene of battle, with a message to General Rutherford at Dickson's plantation, about three miles from the Tuckaseege ford, telling him of his intention to attack next morning and asking his coöperation. Johnston returned to Ramseur's Mill with Rutherford's men, but the battle was over when they arrived.

At King's Mountain Colonel Johnston commanded the reserves which were called into action soon after the battle began.

From that time until the termination of hostilities, he served in many minor capacities requiring bravery.

Several years before the war Colonel Johnston married Jane Ewart, eldest daughter of Robert Ewart, a Scotch-Irish patriot of Mecklenburg County. After his marriage he bought valuable lands on the Catawba River near the present Lincoln County line. To this plantation he returned, and here he spent the rest of his life with his family in the performance of neighborly kindnesses and religious duties. He was a member of Unity Presbyterian Church near the present Gaston-Lincoln line and was a ruling elder for a number of years.

He died July 23, 1805, aged about 63 years. With his wife and other members of his family, he lies buried in a private cemetery on his farm.

His numerous descendants have become useful citizens, many of them attaining places of honor and distinction.

ROBERT HENRY

In the office of the Secretary of State in Raleigh, there is a record of a land grant to Thomas Henry for 168 acres located on the east side of the South Fork of the Catawba, dated September 26, 1766. Twelve years prior to this time, on February 28, 1754, one had been issued to a William Henry down near the confluence of the South Fork and the Catawba. From the two families to which these grants were made sprang the several Gaston County Revolutionary heroes of that name.

It is known that Robert Henry was a son of Thomas Henry, who also saw Revolutionary service. One record states that Robert was born in Tryon County on February 10, 1765; another that he was born in Rowan County in a rail pen. It could easily have been in what was then Tryon County on the South Fork grant, for often lands were settled and entries made long before grants were issued.

His father was from North Ireland and had instilled in his son that patriotism so characteristic of the Scotch-Irish. Robert was one of Major Chronicle's "South Fork boys," and though only sixteen at the time, he displayed such heroism at King's Mountain as to cover himself with undying glory. Near the beginning of the engagement, Major Chronicle was killed. Lieutenant Colonel Ham-

This marker was placed in the Olney Church cemetery in commemoration of Revolutionary War soldiers. It reads: "To the memory of the Revolutionary soldiers and patriots buried in Olney Churchyard" and bears a list of the men's names. (Photo courtesy of the Gaston County Museum of Art and History.)

Hoylesville Post Office, northwest of Dallas. (Photo courtesy of the Gaston County Museum of Art and History.)

The Rhyne home, bearing the date "1799" in its brick. *(Photo courtesy of the Gaston County Museum of Art and History.)*

The Stagecoach House. *(Photo courtesy of the Gaston County Museum of Art and History.)*

bright, now leading the Gaston County men, pressed on and fought with great determination. Before reaching the top of the hill, several of their number were killed by rifle balls. Then the enemy charged bayonet. Robert Henry had placed himself behind a log lying across a hollow and was firing from that position. While he was in the act of cocking his gun, a bayonet glanced along the barrel, passed through one of his hands, and penetrated his thigh. Henry, in the mix-up, shot the Tory. He could not tell how it happened, but supposed that he must have touched the trigger and discharged his rifle. Evidently the ball cut a main artery of his antagonist, as he bled profusely. Henry fell with the Tory to the ground, completely transfixed. Through a mist of powder smoke he saw many of his friends and neighbors, not more than a gun's length ahead of the Tory bayonets. He saw them fire with deadly effect upon their pursuers and retire to the bottom of the hill, quickly reloading and in turn chasing their enemies up the mountain. William Caldwell, another "South Fork boy," seeing Henry's predicament, pulled the bayonet out of his thigh, but finding it still fast in his hand gave the wounded hand a kick with his boot which loosed the instrument from its hold.

Near the end of the battle, Henry, making his way to a branch to quench his thirst, met Colonel Graham on his large black horse, accompanied by David Dicky. After he had started home, he heard the firing and could not resist the temptation to return and take part in the battle. In this he was disappointed, for the fighting was over before he reached the scene. A little girl, Sarah, Colonel Graham's only child, was born that night.

On Saturday evening, after the battle, Robert Henry was taken part of the way to his home on the South Fork. He was taken the remainder of the way on Sunday. Hugh Ewing and Andrew Berry, two of his near neighbors and friends, acted as his escorts. They left him, going on to their own homes for the night. Returning early Monday morning they found him much improved, owing to the effects of a poultice of wet, warm ashes which his mother had applied to his wounds.

While Ewing and Berry were still at the Henry home, several Tories, styling themselves as neutrals, called to learn the news of the battle. Ewing and Berry told them that Ferguson was really killed and his army defeated and taken prisoners. They were certain because they saw him after he was dead. Even the wounded Henry was carried to take a look at him. They told of the meeting near Gilbert Town when between six and seven hundred went on ahead, leaving as many or more footmen to follow, and of the surrounding and defeat of Ferguson. The Tories were slow to believe that so few could have accomplished so much, but Ewing and Berry responded, "We are all of us blue hens' chickens— real fighters and no mistake." The Tories, not believing what they were told, said, "There must have been over four thousand in all. We see what you are about—that your aim is to catch Lord Cornwallis napping."

The above conversation took place not more than two hours after sunrise on Monday, October 9th. The Tories then quickly took their departure. Swimming a horse across the swollen Catawba by the side of a canoe, they hastened to give Cornwallis his first news of Ferguson's defeat.

It was accounts such as these, largely exaggerated by the fear-stricken Tories, which so alarmed the British commander that he sent out Tarleton to aid Ferguson, if still alive, and which finally induced his Lordship to depart from Charlotte with all his army.

Robert Henry was at Cowan's Ford and was near General William Davidson when he was killed.

After the Revolution, Henry became a surveyor. In 1795 he surveyed and made a plot of Matthew Leeper's land on the west bank of the Catawba. This was a part of the James Leeper grant. Another part was sold by James Leeper, a son of the pioneer, to Isaac Henry about the beginning of the nineteenth century. The home site of Isaac was one of the most beautiful along the river. The building has long since fallen into decay, but the loveliness of the spot on a bluff overlooking the stream remains unsurpassed. The place is still known as the Henry lands.

Not until after the Revolution did the white occupation of North Carolina extend beyond the Blue Ridge. Subsequent to that time, among the first to cross and settle in the new county of Buncombe were General Charles McDowell, Colonel David Vance, grandfather of Zebulon B. Vance, and private Robert Henry. Doubtless as a reward for their services at King's Mountain, they were appointed to run and mark the line between North Carolina and Tennessee. McDowell and Vance were commissioners, and Henry was the surveyor. While on this work, Henry wrote the narrative of his own recollections and experiences at King's Mountain and Cowan's Ford. McDowell and Vance also wrote theirs and left them in the care of Henry. After his death, his son, William L. Henry, entrusted the manuscripts to the late Dr. J. F. E. Hanly who sent them to Dr. Lyman C. Draper of Wisconsin. On the facts contained therein was largely based his Draper's "King's Mountain and its Heroes," published in 1880. This publication has been frequently drawn upon for incidents of the battle. After he completed his work as surveyor on the Tennessee-North Carolina line, Robert Henry studied law and was licensed to practice in July, 1802. He developed into a very able man and left his impress upon Buncombe County and Western North Carolina, where he spent his later years. He died on January 6, 1863, aged 98 years. He was the last of the heroes of King's Mountain.

To him we are indebted for the preservation and part authorship of the most graphic and detailed account of the battles of King's Mountain and Cowan's Ford which now exist.

On page 97 of John Preston Arthur's "History of Western North Carolina" is a picture of Robert Henry from a daguerrotype made in his 94th year.

MOSES HENRY

Among the early settlers of Gaston County, it is known that there were two families of Henrys, those of Thomas and William. Ten years prior to the time that Thomas, the father of Robert, settled on the South Fork, William Henry had established a home on a tract of 600 acres of land granted him, February 28, 1754, near the junction of the South Fork and Catawba Rivers. On the South Carolina border near King's Mountain there were other Henrys, among them "Big Jim," noted for his pugilistic tendencies. But it was the South Point Henrys who added splendor to the illustrious deeds of King's Mountain.

William Henry, said by the records to have sold much leather to the army, was the father of Moses, James, and perhaps others.

Moses Henry married Margaret, only child of John and Rebecca Clark Baldriech, who lived not far from the Henry home, back of the plantation now known as the Rosa McLean place. After their marriage prior to or during the Revolution, they left the immediate neighborhood of their kin and established a home on Crowder's Creek where Henry ran a gristmill. He was engaged in this occupation when the urge of patriotism caused him to leave his wife and small children alone on the farm, join his former comrades of the South Fork and go to the defense of his country at King's Mountain where he fell mortally wounded on the field of battle. He was carried to a Charlotte hospital where he soon died in spite of the tender ministrations of Dr. William McLean, a friend and neighbor.

He lies buried in Charlotte, the site of his grave unknown. Walton Hand, a great grandson, says he was buried in Charlotte.

Rebecca, a daughter of Moses Henry and Margaret Baldriech Henry, married Aaron Hand and became the ancestress of the Hand families of Lowell, Belmont, and many other places to which they have gone. They have rendered patriotism in time of peace as conspicuously as their ancestor served on a field of war.

Mrs. Price Rankin of Gastonia, a descendant, has in her possession a pair of Moses Henry's knee buckles and a bowl, which were family possessions.

After Henry's death, Margaret, the widow, continued to run the mill in order to make a living for herself and children. She was a brave woman, afraid of nothing but Tories with which the community was infested. It was sometimes necessary to hide herself and children from them and often necessary to hide food, especially butter, among the rocks of the mill dam to keep the Tories from carrying it away. She was married the second time to Jonathan Gullick, the Gaston County pioneer of that name and ancestor of the Gullicks of the county. There were several children by this marriage, all of whom moved to Tennessee except Milton, who stayed behind to take care of his mother who refused to go.

Jonathan Gullick was the first person buried in New Hope graveyard. Twelve or thirteen years later his wife died at the age of 93 and sleeps by his side. Hers was the second grave in the cemetery.

JOHN CHITTIM

John Chittim was a son of William Chittim who lived on what is still known as the Chittim bottoms on Catawba Creek, just back of the home of William McLean on the New Hope road. In the office of the Secretary of State in Raleigh, there is a record of the original grant to this land issued to William Chittim, December 23, 1763, on the northeast side of the South Fork of the Catawba. It is now owned by the Duke Power Company and the children of Mrs. Rosa McLean.

During the Revolution John Chittim was a private in the company of Captain Samuel Martin. This was but natural since the families were near neighbors on Catawba Creek. He was with his captain at King's Mountain. After the death of Major Chronicle and William Rabb, the Lincoln men pressed on under their officers. Before they reached the crest of the mountain the enemy fired their guns and then charged bayonet, killing Captain Mattocks and John Boyd and wounding William Gilmer and John Chittim. Chittim was shot in the side and this made an ugly wound. Yet he fully recovered and lived to a good old age.

He was placed on the invalid pension roll in 1815 and drew seventy-two dollars a year for three years until his death, December 24, 1818, thirty-eight years after being wounded.

He is buried in the cemetery of Bethel Presbyterian Church.

ELISHA WITHERS OR WEATHERS

Elisha Withers was born in Virginia on August
10, 1762, a son of John Withers, the pioneer
with whom he came to Gaston County prior to the
Revolution. They settled a short distance from
where Long Creek Baptist Church now stands.

At the age of eighteen he began his first military
service, acting as commissary in furnishing provis-
ions for the soldiers stationed at Captain Robert
Alexander's place near the Tuckaseege ford on the
Catawba River. Later he was drafted and served in
other capacities.

He was not present at King's Mountain because
he was afflicted with smallpox at the time of the
battle. Hearing the guns, he left his sickbed and
went to the spring where he stayed until the firing
ceased.

He married Sarah, the daughter of Francis
Gascoigne, Gaskin, or Gaston, as the Welch name
was spelled at different periods. Gascoigne settled,
lived, and died near Lowell.

Elisha Withers was highly respected. He lived
to a good old age and is buried by the side of his
wife in the cemetery of the church near which he
made his home.

JAMES WITHERSPOON

James Witherspoon, pioneer and later a Revolutionary soldier, was born in Londonderry, Ireland,
in 1747. He came to Gaston County before the

Revolution and entered 640 acres of land about three miles south of Sandy Plains Baptist Church. For this land he later obtained a grant from King George III.

Having secured title for a home site, he returned to Ireland for his wife and three children. His wife died shortly after landing. He then married, in 1776, Mrs. Elinor Beard Black, a widow with six children. The line of descent for his Gaston County progeny was through Annie Graham Witherspoon, a child of his second marriage, whose husband was James Lewis.

James Witherspoon was a captain in the Revolution. He was captured and taken prisoner to Camden, South Carolina. While he was in prison, his wife took their baby, Annie Graham Witherspoon, and went to visit him. Upon arrival she inquired for her husband, who heard her voice and asked if she would know him if she saw him. After the visit, he and two other prisoners slipped by the guards, swam the river, and came near his home where his wife carried food to him in his hiding place.

Honored and revered by his descendants for his faithful performance of duty, he peacefully sleeps by the side of his second wife, Elinor Black Witherspoon, in the cemetery of Olney Presbyterian Church. He died July 8, 1838, at the ripe old age of 91 years, having outlived his wife who died in 1834. She was born in 1741.

An old chest with rings, through which a rope was placed to lash it to the mast of the ship, made three trips with him across the ocean and is still in possession of a member of the family. The Lewises, Smyres, Durhams, Kendricks, some of the Fords and Wilsons, the James P. Stowes, and many others of the county are among his descendants.

The above information was furnished, for the most part, by the late Miss Mary Lewis of Gastonia.

ANDREW BERRY

Almost nothing is known of Andrew Berry except that he was a Revolutionary soldier, the son of Hugh and Margaret Berry, and that he was one of three boys of the South Point section of Gaston whose names were linked together after the battle of King's Mountain. The three were Robert Henry, Hugh Ewing, and Andrew Berry, all mere youths. Robert Henry was badly wounded. His two friends brought him to his home on the South Fork. Starting on Saturday after the battle they arrived the next day. Sunday they left Henry in the care of his mother and went to their own homes near by for the night, returning early the next morning to learn of the condition of their comrade. While at the Henry home, the conversation with the Tories took place. This is recorded in the sketch of Robert Henry on page 137. The dates of his death and age are found on his tombstone in old Goshen graveyard where he peacefully sleeps with a group of his kindred. This family group helps to substantiate the tradition that among the few English coming to the county before the Revolution and settling on the Catawba near Belmont were the Berrys or Barrys—the name is spelled both ways on tombstones——, the Shipleys, and the Lincolns, and that Abraham, the father of Tom Lincoln, was among them and that while here he married Mary Shipley and to them were born, here in Gaston County, three children, Mordacai, Josiah, and Thomas. Later Abraham Lincoln and some of the Shipleys and Berrys moved to Kentucky where Abraham Lincoln and his wife, Mary Shipley, had two other children, Mary and Nancy. Mary married a Crum and Nancy a Branfield, as history records.

Tradition has it that Tom Lincoln, always a wanderer, came back from Kentucky to visit his kinsfolk, the Shipleys and Berrys, and met Nancy Hanks. The Hankses had been neighbors to the Shipleys, Berrys, and Lincolns in Virginia. What was more natural than for Nancy Hanks, after joining her relatives in Kentucky, to marry Tom Lincoln, whom she had known in North Carolina.

Were it possible to turn back the pages of time, happenings of great interest would be revealed.

HUGH EWING

On hills and bluffs overlooking the Catawba and South Fork Rivers, many places of unparalleled scenic beauty were the homes of Gaston County pioneers. Along the banks of these rivers moved the first settlers of the county, and near them their descendants have lived through all the changing years. During the Revolution, when the call of patriotism came to them, they answered nobly, though many of them were mere youths who followed their leaders in epoch-making battles.

One such settlement was that of the Ewings on a hillside near the present location of the Stowe Thread Mill of Belmont. The spring from which the family used water was in the creek bottom near by.

Hugh Ewing, a son of the pioneer George Ewing, was a Revolutionary soldier, who, though only seventeen or eighteen years old, took part in the battle of King's Mountain. After the battle Hugh Ewing and Andrew Berry brought home Robert Henry, a youthful companion, who was badly wounded. An account of this is given in a sketch of Robert Henry.

George Ewing was the Scotch-Irish father of Hugh. He was also a Revolutionary soldier who is mentioned in Colonial Records as being a road overseer, as serving in the Revolution during the last year of the war, and as receiving army pay.

When the first census was taken in 1790, George was head of a family of four females. Hugh at that time was also head of a family. The names were listed near together, which proves that Hugh lived near by. No mention is made of other sons.

Hugh Ewing reared a large family of three sons, Samuel, Robert, and Hugh, and three daughters, Margaret who married a Gingles, Sallie who married James Allison, and Polly who married a Davis. All of these, with the possible exception of Polly, settled on paternal lands.

Two granddaughters, Mrs. Will Abee and Mrs. Julius Abee, are still living near Belmont. In the home of Mrs. Julius Abee is the old family Bible, printed in Edinburgh, Scotland, in 1752. It is yellowed with age, but fairly well preserved. The Bible records the birth of Hugh which was on March 2, 1762. He was married February 2, 1786, six years after he fought at King's Mountain. He died in 1824 and is buried in Goshen graveyard.

MATTHEW LEEPER

Matthew Leeper was born May 27, 1755, the son of James Leeper, pioneer and owner of large tracts of land on the Catawba River. James Leeper had at least two sons, Matthew and James, Jr. Matthew, being the elder, upon the death of his father, inherited his lands. He later deeded 300 acres to his brother James, the consideration being natural love and affection.

The location of the home site is about two and one-half miles southeast of Belmont, though the plantation extended considerably farther down the river. The old log home of Matthew Leeper is still standing near what has for years been known as the Leeper Gold Mine.

Matthew was a "South Fork boy" who served in the Revolutionary War, taking part in the battle of King's Mountain. He died October 12, 1849, in his 95th year and is buried in Smith's graveyard near Belmont. The writer's father, the late C. T. Stowe, then a boy of sixteen, remembered the old man and had talked with him.

JAMES HENRY

Not much is known of James Henry, a brother of Moses Henry, except that he fought bravely at

King's Mountain and that a few days later, lured by unstilled memories, returned to the scene of the conflict and while wandering on the wooded hills found a very fine horse handsomely equipped, evidently having belonged to a British officer. Young Henry thought his luck good, but his patriotic mother met him at the gate when he took it home and sternly told him to turn it loose and drive it off the place; for, said she, "I will not have the hands of my household soiled with British plunder."

MATTHEW ARMSTRONG

Matthew Armstrong, Revolutionary soldier, was a son of John Armstrong of Scotch descent, the pioneer of that name in the southeastern part of the county. On August 30, 1753, he obtained a grant for 350 acres on what is now the Belmont side of the South Fork at Armstrong's Ford, later Armstrong's Bridge. The first home of the family was near the highway on the right hand side going toward the South Fork. It was built of massive logs still preserved, in a barn, on the farm of the late Jasper Armstrong.

Matthew Armstrong, then only eighteen years of age, was one of Chronicle's "South Fork boys" and fought at King's Mountain and the Cowpens.

The late A. J. Smith, Register of Deeds of Gaston County and a student of history, often spoke of the shot-torn hat which his grandfather, Matthew Armstrong, wore at King's Mountain and held out on his gun to draw the fire of the enemy before stepping from behind a tree to return fire.

The above facts were furnished by the late Miss M. Ella Armstrong, one of Matthew's descendants, who was for years a teacher in an Alabama college.

Matthew Armstrong married Mrs. Margaret Shipley Sloan of Mecklenburg County, by whom he had several children. They were the ancestors of many now living in the county.

He was born in 1762 and died June 21, 1838, and is buried by the side of his wife in Smith's graveyard near Belmont.

JOHN MCLEAN

John McLean was another Gaston County soldier of the Revolution who gave his life for freedom's cause. He was a son of Alexander McLean and a brother of Dr. William McLean. Born in Rowan County, he was brought by his parents when a very small child to the South Point section of Gaston, where he grew up with his brothers and sisters on his father's plantation. When the call to serve his country came to him, he joined the Rutherford regiment and was in the seige of Charleston. There he was taken prisoner, but was paroled and permitted to return home. In the same year he joined a company under Captain Osborne and was sent with a party to examine the position of the British at Buford Bridge (Beaufort County). During a skirmish at that place he was shot in the head and killed while attempting, from behind a tree, to shoot a sentry. He was in the service three months, for which he was to have received one-half bushel of salt. This was given to his brother, Thomas, by Captain Osborne.

SAMUEL CALDWELL

A family of Caldwells came to old Tryon, now Gaston County, in 1772, and settled where Belmont Abbey College now stands. They were from Orange County where at least one of the boys, Samuel, was born on February 10, 1759. This made him thirteen years old at the time of his pioneering here, likely with his parents.

When very young, Samuel became interested in military affairs, and in 1776 in Captain Gowen's company he fought Cherokee Indians beyond the mountains. In 1779 he volunteered for nine months' service in the company of his near neighbor, William Chronicle. The company joined General Lincoln's regiment at Purysburg, S. C. He participated in the battle of King's Mountain as a member of Captain Isaac White's company. He fought at the Cowpens and Guilford Court House, and continued in active service until the close of the war.

When the fighting was over he married Miss Elizabeth Gullick, sister of Jonathan Gullick, Gaston County pioneer of that name, and settled as a farmer on home lands where he reared a large family noted in the community for its intelligence and also for its devilment. Many stories are still told of pranks played by them; sometimes at the expense of others, sometimes themselves.

Samuel was a member of Goshen Church and is buried in its old cemetery with others of his kin.

Although his sons and grandsons married and settled near him, the family is now widely scattered and the name is practically extinct in the community where it once played so prominent a part.

WILLIAM CALDWELL

William Caldwell, a brother of Samuel, was also a Revolutionary soldier and participated in the battle of King's Mountain. His services there seem to have been more in helping his neighbors than in killing British and Tories. When Robert Henry who lived near him was transfixed by a bayonet, Caldwell pulled it from his hand and thigh, thus releasing Henry from a perilous situation. After the death of Major Chronicle, it was he who brought home Chronicle's horse and placed it in his father's stable without telling the family. Next morning when Mr. Chronicle found the horse he knew his son was dead.

William Caldwell lived near the present town of Belmont for several years after the war.

The date and place of his death are uncertain.

OLD MAN CALDWELL AND ABE COLLINS

An interesting story is told of the part played by an old Mr. Caldwell in the winning of the battle of King's Mountain. The old man, whose first name is unknown, lived in the forks of the Catawba on the direct road to the Tuckaseege ford and Charlotte. Since this was the location of the home of Samuel and William Caldwell, it seems pretty certain that the old gentleman was their father.

When Colonel Patrick Ferguson, encamped on a spur of King's Mountain, learned of the advancing mountaineers and their allies, he felt insecure, but, scorning retreat, sent an express to Cornwallis at Charlotte asking for immediate aid. Abe Collins, a notorious Tory leader and counterfeiter who lived near the South Carolina border, was the messenger chosen. Hardly had Collins started before word was passed, by grapevine telegraph, to the patriots of the South Fork to be on the lookout for an express. So Mr. Caldwell was not surprised when a dusty rider on a panting steed stopped at his door and asked for food, which was given him. Collins was then made a prisoner and searched. On his person were found the dispatches in which Ferguson begged his commanding officer for aid.

Had Cornwallis received the letter and the reenforcements been sent, the Whigs would have been trapped by Tarleton on one side and by Ferguson on the mountain.

For three days Abe Collins was kept a prisoner in the Caldwell home. He reached Charlotte three days after Ferguson's army had been defeated and he had been killed.

Though so largely responsible for the glorious victory at King's Mountain, there is only a fleeting glimpse of Mr. Caldwell as he passes uncertainly across the pages of history.

JAMES GLENN

James Glenn was born in Berkely County, Virginia, in 1759 and came to Gaston County before the Revolutionary War with his father, John Glenn, and other members of the family. The first settlement, so far as known, was near Lowell at what is now called the Becky Matthews' place.

When very young he began military service as a private, substituting for his father in state troops under General Rutherford who was fighting Cherokee Indians. Later, as a voluntary mounted rifleman, he arrested and brought to trial many Tories who had returned to the state from Ninety-Six, South Carolina. Completing this duty, he spent one month guarding the frontier from Indians. After rendering further service as a mounted rifleman, he took part in the battle of King's Mountain and then spent three months under Captain Thomas Loftin with whom he started to Wilmington, but was ordered back. He spent the remainder of his enlistment, to 1781, chasing Tories.

After the war he moved to the upper part of York County, South Carolina, where he reared a family of twelve children, as follows: Jane McLean; John, who married Sarah Johnston; James Erwin; William, who married Eliza Boyd; Henry, who married Jane Brown; Robert, who married Parmela McGill; Polly, who married David Johnston; Samuel, who married Miss Reid; Franklin, who married Polly Craig; Eliza Adelaide, who married Whiting Stowe; Wilson, who married Mary Hendrick; and Martha, who married Warren Hendrick.

Many of his descendants are still living in this
and adjoining counties: the Glenns, of Gastonia
and elsewhere; the Rankins, who descended from
Major Rufus and Sarah Stowe Rankin; the Beatys;
the Mary Johnston Armstrongs; Janie Johnston
Howe, from whom this material was obtained; and
many others.

James Glenn became a pensioner in 1833. He
lived to a ripe old age and is buried at Bethel.

JAMES RUTLEDGE

James Rutledge was the son of George Rutledge,
the pioneer of that name in the Mt. Holly section.
George was an extensive land owner; some parcels
were obtained by grant, others by purchase. A
part of this land lying on Dutchman's Creek above
Stanley became the farm home of James.

He was a Revolutionary soldier, serving as a private in Captain John Johnston's company, Colonel
John Collier's regiment, N. C. militia.

The following story is credited to Charles Smith
of Stanley, son of Milton Smith, who was noted for
his knowledge of local historical events: When Cornwallis was camped at Flat Rock between Lincolnton and Denver, he sent out foraging parties. One
came down Dutchman's Creek to the Rutledge plantation, but was stopped and driven back by the
Rutledge boys, mere children too young to go to
the army. By hiding and shooting from different
places, they gave the impression of strength they
did not possess. The British were driven back

across the creek and lost one man. Nothing was taken from the farm that day.

James Rutledge was three times married. He was an elder in Goshen Presbyterian Church and lies buried in the old graveyard there.

George Rutledge, a brother of James, was also a Revolutionary soldier. He went to Tennessee after the war.

GEORGE OLIVER

If the traveler along the Wilkinson Boulevard will observe closely, he will see an old house site a short distance from the Cramerton bridge on the Belmont side of the river. Here stood the home of George Oliver, a Revolutionary soldier and one of the "South Fork boys." The highway is directly over where the house stood. The old yard is overgrown with wild lespedeza, and one or two old-fashioned rose bushes are still standing on opposite sides of the road, showing the location of both back and front yards. Down the hill from the back is a bold spring. A white oak now grows over it. Two old walnut trees are there and near by some tall, straight poplars, the growth of much more recent years. The house was still standing in the memory of some now living. It had the traditional eight-foot fireplace which took in the logs as hauled from the woods without cutting.

Just before the bridge is reached, an old roadway, emerging from the woods, is lost under the macadam to come into view again on the opposite side. It may be traced through the forest to the water's edge of the South Fork. This was known as the Oliver's Ford Road and leads to Oliver's Ford, a noted river crossing in the old days. It was named for the Revolutionary patriot, George Oliver. In Gaston County are still living some of his descendants. He was the great grandfather of George McKee and his sister, Mrs. W. R. Rankin, of near Belmont. George Oliver and his wife, Sarah, are buried in the Goshen graveyard in plainly marked graves. The inscription on his tombstone proves him to have been a very young man during his Revolutionary experiences. Indeed he was a "South Fork boy."

JOHN HOFFMAN

John Hoffman, Revolutionary soldier, was born in Germany in 1760 and came with his father, Jacob Hoffman, the pioneer, and other members of the family from the upper Rhine country of Germany. They landed in Philadelphia and settled first in Pennsylvania, later coming to North Carolina. They located in the German section of Gaston County at the junction of Leeper's and Killian's Creeks.

John, though only a boy when the Revolutionary War broke out, entered the service under Lieutenant Colonel Hambright and with him engaged in occasional expeditions. This continued until the battle of King's Mountain, in which conflict he was wounded. Miles and John Hoffman, two grandsons, testified that they saw the scar made by a

British bullet which plowed through the skin almost straight across his breast.

After the close of the war he married Margaret Hovis, daughter of George Hovis, the Gaston County pioneer of that name. They lived two miles southeast of Dallas, near Big Long Creek.

He is described as a man of character, diligent in business and skilled in all sorts of mechanical work. He became prosperous. But more than houses and lands, he valued his family. When his wife died on August 18, 1832, his grief was inconsolable and in shortly more than a month, September 24, 1832, he also died and was laid by her side. They were buried in a private graveyard on their home place.

John Hoffman had one brother, Jacob, born in Germany, with whom he often talked of the hardships of the ocean voyage. He also had four sisters: Elizabeth, Mary, Hannah, and Catharine.

WILLIAM RANKIN

William Rankin was a son of Samuel and Ellen Alexander Rankin. He was born in Pennsylvania about 1760 and when two or three years old was brought, in 1763, by his family to the settlement on Dutchman's Creek. Two years later the family moved to a large tract of land which was granted to his father between Stanley and Dutchman's Creeks. The settlement has long been known as Rankintown.

When just a boy, he entered military service as a private in the company of his uncle, Robert Alexander, Colonel William Graham's regiment. Several times he volunteered for some specific service. The first time was in an uprising against the Cherokee Indians. Then he went to the relief of Charleston with the Lincoln regiment. Finding that city completely surrounded by the British army, the regiment returned home. Again, in 1780, he volunteered to help drive the Tories from upper South Carolina. After that he came home for a little while, but was too much of a patriot to remain idle with his country needing him so much. Therefore, he joined the forces encamped on Colonel Dickson's plantation near Tuckaseege. Early in the morning of June 20, 1780, they broke camp and marched to Ramseur's Mill to put down the Tories who were assembled there in a large body under Colonel John Moore. They reached the scene two hours after the battle had taken place. For a while he continued to fight the troublesome Tories, and then marched with General Rutherford's command to Camden and participated in that unfortunate battle. He watched the movements of the British army in Charlotte, and later took part in the battle of Eutaw Springs. After that he was sent to Salisbury with a large number of prisoners, where he remained until discharged.

Colonel Richard Rankin, father of Rev. Frank B. Rankin, of the county, and Mrs. Kathleen Rankin Moore, of Gastonia, was a son of William and lived in the house now occupied by Rev. Frank B. Rankin. It was built in 1800 by William Rankin. Just to the rear of this house, still standing in a good state of preservation, William previously built another house in 1789 on a three hundred acre tract deeded him by his father, Samuel Rankin. The William Rankin house stands within a few hundred yards of the original Samuel Rankin settlement.

In 1789 William Rankin married Mary Moore, a sister of General John Moore. He lived to be nearly 93 years old and is said to have been the last surviving soldier of the Revolution in Gaston County.

PETER EDDLEMAN

Peter Eddleman was the youngest son of Bostian and Sarah Eddleman, who came to this country from Germany and settled first in Pennsylvania. Later, when Peter was very young, they moved to North Carolina where they established their home on the Gaston County side of what is now the Lincoln-Gaston line in the historic Macpelah Church section.

Peter was born May 19, 1762. When only a boy, he joined the Revolutionary forces as a private under General Forney. He was in many engagements, among them the battle of the Cowpens, and was present at the surrender at Yorktown.

After the war he settled on his large farm in the Gastonia Grove Church locality. A part of the farm near Lucia is now owned by W. P. Eddleman, a grandson of Peter. He is one of the few grandsons or granddaughters of Revolutionary soldiers now living in the county.

While he owned and lived on a large plantation and could have been styled a planter, his fame rests upon the cabinetmakers' trade in which he became very efficient. Some fine examples of his work are still in existence and have become priceless heirlooms for which large sums have been refused. His carving and inlay work were exceptionally beautiful. No nails were used in his cabinets and no metal except the H and L hinges which were hand-wrought.

Peter Eddleman lived a bachelor until he was 68 years old when he married a widow, Mrs. Dica Swanson Clippard. To the union were born two sons, David Franklin and William Peter. The late Dr. H. M. Eddleman, of Gastonia, and W. P. Eddleman, of the county, were children of David.

Peter Eddleman died on May 19, 1847, and is buried in the old Whitehouse burying ground in Lincoln County. He was a man of unusual ability.

COLONEL CHARLES MCLEAN

Colonel Charles McLean became prominently identified with both the civil and military life of Tryon, now Gaston County, prior to and during the Revolution. This will be shown by the following sketch taken from material loaned by the late Rear Admiral Ridley McLean, U. S. N., Washington, D. C., a descendant, and from the Colonial Records.

He was of another family of McLeans than that to which the South Fork McLeans belonged. He was accompanied to America by a brother, Ephraim, and a cousin, John, who may have been the John to whom a grant was issued on Long Creek, date not given. Ephraim was born in 1730. Charles was two or three years older. The place of birth of neither

is known. The wife of Charles was Susannah Howard Allison, widow of Thomas Allison, of Pennsylvania, with whom she fled to the Carolinas after
a severe quarrel with her father, Dr. Howard, of
Philadelphia. The following estimation of her
character is taken from a letter written by a grandson, the Hon. Finis Ewing McLean, in 1875: "My
grandmother, whose maiden name was Susan Howard, was a most extraordinary woman, one of the
noblest and most self-sacrificing of the American
Revolution. She sent three sons, Samuel and Robert
Allison and John McLean, into the war at its
beginning. They fought to the end. Not only this,
but she joined my grandfather, Charles McLean,
most heartily, in selling their large estate to maintain
the soldiers and the credit of the American government. She was the daughter and only child, by his
first wife, of Dr. Howard, who was quite wealthy.
Reared in affluence, highly educated and greatly
beloved by her parents, proud and high spirited,
she never bore insult or oppression. She lost her
mother when about sixteen years of age. Her father
soon married again, a woman who became a tyran-
nical stepmother with whom Susannah could not
get along. In the family jars that resulted, the father
sided with the stepmother and one day reprimanded
Susannah in the street when she, under great excite-
ment, held up her hand and declared she would
leave home and that she would marry the first man
who asked her to become his wife. Across the street
there worked a fine looking blacksmith, who, without seeking her acquaintance, had long admired her

beauty and worth. He overheard her. As soon as the father went into the house the blacksmith, Allison by name, stepped up and claimed that he was the first to ask her to marry him. She replied that she would never go back on her word. They were married and fled to Carolina, where her husband died within a few years leaving her with two small boys, Samuel and Robert."

She afterwards married Charles McLean. According to family records, this marriage occurred in South Carolina, probably in the vicinity of Allison Creek, where McLean purchased a tract of 400 acres of land in 1765. There is a record of the sale of this land the next year. Susannah McLean's name appeared in the deed as one of the parties to the transaction.

After having sold his York County holdings, he made several purchases on the North Fork of Crowder's Creek, which was his home throughout the Revolution and up to the time of his migration to Kentucky in 1797.

From 1766 to 1780 there is a fairly continuous record of Charles McLean, appearing in land transactions and in civil and military service during the Revolution. Deeds recording land sales show that he sold an aggregate of 500 acres during 1779-80. The reason for the sale is said to have been: "When he found the finances of the Colonies almost exhausted and their soldiers in tatters and rags he sold his possessions and loaned the proceeds to the Federal government, accepting therefor a note signed by a committee, many of whom were signers of the

Mecklenburg Declaration of Independence." At that time there was no Treasury Department. The above transaction was made with the full approval of McLean's wife. It is said that they never regretted their action and, though passing their later years in reduced circumstances, they never made effort to recover repayment of their assistance.

At the outbreak of the Revolution he was about 48 years old with a wife and three children and two grown stepsons, Samuel and Robert Allison. He was living on a farm of about five or six hundred acres on the upper branch of Crowder's Creek near Crowder's Mountain and only three or four miles from the celebrated King's Mountain. Some of his outstanding activities follow. He was one of three commissioners to select the site of Tryon County Court House. In June, 1775, after the boundary dispute between North Carolina and South Carolina was settled, many people having land grants in North Carolina became very uneasy lest they should be taken from them by new entries from South Carolina. Charles McLean was one of a hundred to petition the King to prevent this. The inhabitants of Tryon County early organized committees of safety to protect themselves against the acts and methods of the Mother country. Charles McLean was a charter member of the first of these committees. It was this committee which adopted what is now known as the Tryon County Declaration of Rights and Independence from British Tyranny. It was signed by Charles McLean, John

Walker, and forty-six others. On September 9, 1775, he appears, for the first time, to have been appointed to military rank. This appears in Colonial Records of N. C., Vol. 10, p. 206. It is recorded in the Council Journal of the Provincial Congress held at Hillsboro that Charles McLean of Tryon County was made Lieutenant Colonel of militia. He was a member of the Provincial Congress at Halifax during April and May, 1776. In 1777 he commanded the first regiment which marched from Tryon County against the Tories of upper South Carolina. Rank and pride didn't play much part when duty confronted Revolutionary heroes. After Charles McLean had been duly commissioned Lieutenant Colonel, we find him major of the 2nd battalion of militia of the Salisbury district. In April of the same year as his activities against the S. C. Tories, he was a member of the General Assembly held at New Bern, serving on various committees. He introduced a bill for appointing a committee to build a court house, prison, and stocks for the County of Tryon. He had previously served on a committee for selecting the court house site. The bill passed and the committee was named. He was apparently at no time in the regular army. His services were with the militia or with the unorganized units which were so frequent in those days. Many men of this section went out when needed, as at Ramseur's Mill and King's Mountain.

There is recorded (Vol. 14, N. C. State Records, pp. 261-262) a letter from Charles McLean to the

General Assembly, which indicates the extent of the Tory movement and illustrates the importance of necessary forces to quell it. This letter was written from Crowder's Mountain, Tryon County, on February 6, 1779. He mentions their boastfulness that they would soon be masters of the country and his own diligence in raising a regiment, through God's assistance, to stop their ravages and prevent their strengthening the British army. In another letter without date, but evidently written about one year before the battle of King's Mountain, with heading Lincoln County (it will be remembered that Tryon was divided into Lincoln and Rutherford in 1779), Charles McLean, using very quaint language, resigned his commission as colonel of the Lincoln regiment and volunteered as a private. The fact that this regiment engaged in the battle of King's Mountain under the leadership of Major Chronicle and Lieutenant Colonel Hambright, who took the place of Colonel William Graham, the man who obviously succeeded McLean, would indicate that the letter mentioned above marked the end of his military services as an officer. The fact that he is said, by family tradition, to have carried to his death certain wounds received at King's Mountain and that official records do not mention him as an officer in that battle shows that his letter was no idle gesture, but that this patriot, then over fifty years of age, did at that time take up his musket in freedom's cause.

In the first census taken in 1790, Charles McLean appears as a householder in Lincoln County. In his home at that time were two males over sixteen, one female, and five slaves. The second male was doubt-less his son, John, who died soon after from the effects of wounds and exposure during the war. Another householder shown in the census was Ephraim McLean, his son. This family had one male under sixteen, who was Ephraim's son, John, born February, 1790. Family records show that in 1796 or 1797 Charles McLean and his wife, Susannah, their orphaned grandson, Charles M. White, and their son, Ephraim, his wife and their three male children, journeyed to Logan County, Kentucky. Here he took up lands, settled, and lived for a few years. He died between 1800 and 1805.

Susannah Howard Allison McLean lived several years after the death of her husband. Owing to the absence of doctors in the entire region of Kentucky to which they went, this brave, fearless woman in her declining years took up the practice of medicine, having acquired a certain knowledge of it from her father, and continued it up to her death.

No records show that her two sons by her first marriage, Samuel and Robert Allison, accompanied the family to Kentucky. They likely became the ancestors of the Allisons of Gaston and York Coun-ties. Susannah Allison McLean died in 1812 and was buried by the side of her husband on the land acquired by them in Kentucky.

The Nancy Hanks marker is still
standing today. It designates the site
of the Dicky Hanks cabin, where the
mother of Abraham Lincoln spent
much of her childhood. Situated within the Pinsto Forest development
off Highway 273 South in Belmont, the marker is seventy-five to one
hundred feet off the Nancy Hanks Place cul-de-sac, which is a right
extension off Dorie Drive. (Photo by Rick Haithcox Photography.)

CHAPTER XII

THE CLOSE OF THE REVOLUTION

After the battle of the Cowpens on the 17th of June, 1781, Lord Cornwallis left his headquarters at Winnsboro, S. C., and marched rapidly to overtake General Morgan on his way to a place of safety in Virginia. He crossed the North Carolina line January 23, 1781, and passed through the present County of Gaston and camped at Tryon Court House.

Tarleton's cavalry also passed through to join Cornwallis, plundering as it went. At the home of Benjamin Ormand on the headwaters of Long Creek, horses were taken. Even the blanket from the baby's cradle was used for a saddle blanket and the old family Bible was stolen for a saddle. The Bible, not being exceedingly comfortable, was discarded at Beatty's ford on the Catawba and later returned to its owner.

Not long after this came the surrender at Yorktown. The men of lower Lincoln, now Gaston, who had fought so valiantly at King's Mountain and other places, were back at their farming again, much alone with their work and their memories. An occasional new neighbor broke the monotony of their lives. A member of one of these families was destined to gain national and international fame— Nancy Hanks, the mother of Abraham Lincoln.

There were busy times on the farms; sheep, cattle, and hogs were raised. Crops were mainly for the families and their cattle. Not much cotton was produced. There was only a small patch on each farm. The women and children picked the seeds by hand. This was usually done after supper when the day's work was over. Next it was spun and woven into cloth.

About 1830 cotton began to be grown in much greater quantities. Many colored families were brought in to help in its production. The people were now thinking and planning how to use it more profitably. They were also thinking of the long distance to the county seat at Lincolnton. Plans were beginning to form in their minds and a determination in their hearts to have a smaller county of their own and a more convenient courthouse.

The people had their way. A new county was established. To this territory, almost a wilderness, new privileges and new responsibilities had come. Farming was almost the only industry, but more lands were needed to be cleared. There were no more log rollings and burnings; lumber was needed for buildings and the sawmill industry developed and expanded. Iron and tin mines had been opened in the northern part of the county. A smelting plant had long been in operation at High Shoals, and gold mines were crudely worked in most sections. Neighbors lived far apart and the roads were bad, in winter almost impassable. These were some of the conditions when the new county came into existence.

CHAPTER XIII

Among the Scotch-Irish pioneers of the southern part of the county were a few English, but for the most part the English came during and after the Revolutionary War. They were attracted, as were the Scotch-Irish, by the beauty and fertility of the Catawba valley. They, too, built their cabins on the bluffs overlooking the stream.

Among those of English stock were the Hankses. Benjamin Hanks, the first of the family, so far as is known, to come to this country, settled in Massachusetts in 1699. One of his sons, William Hanks, moved to Virginia. William had twelve children whose descendants formed a large community in Amelia County. From there they again migrated. Part came to what is now Gaston County, North Carolina, where some of their descendants are still living in Belmont, Gastonia, Dallas, and other places. Others went to Kentucky.

There is proof that several other English families came here with the Hankses or joined them later, afterwards going to Kentucky where some of their relatives and friends were already making their home.

Well-founded tradition says: "The Lincoln and Hanks families were fellow Quakers in Pennsylvania where they lived awhile before going to Virginia. From there Abraham Lincoln, father of

Thomas Lincoln, and other emigrants, including Hankses, Berrys, and Shipleys, came to North Carolina and settled on the Catawba River. The 1790 census locates them in Gaston County, then Lincoln. In the Shipley family were six girls, one of whom, Mary Shipley, married Abraham, father of Thomas Lincoln. Richard Berry married Rachel Shipley, another of the sisters.

"Abraham Lincoln and wife had three children born in North Carolina: Mordacai, Josiah, and Thomas, the husband of Nancy Hanks. Later, Lincoln, with some of the Shipleys and Berrys, emigrated to Kentucky. There Lincoln and his wife had two other children, Mary and Nancy Lincoln."

There are many descendants of the Shipley women, of other names, now living in Gaston County. A large group of Berrys are buried in Goshen graveyard. One of them, Andrew Berry, was a Revolutionary soldier.

The time the Hankses reached this section is obscure, but it is known positively that James Hanks was here as early as 1779. In that year there is a record in the "Marriage Bonds of Tryon and Lincoln Counties, N. C." that James Hanks married Mary Starret. He was still living in the county and was head of a family when the first census was taken in 1790. Richard, or "Dicky Hanks" as he was called, was also living in the county and was head of a family at the same time. When the census was taken the names of the two, supposed to have been brothers, were listed close together in what was called the 11th company of Lincoln County in the

Morgan district. This is positive proof that they lived near together and in the South Point section. "Dicky Hanks" was an uncle of Nancy Hanks, the mother of Abraham Lincoln. She made her home with him on one of the bluffs overlooking the Catawba. The site of the cabin was often pointed out to the writer by her father, C. T. Stowe, who later came into possession of the land. It is now owned by a son, Samuel Pinckney Stowe, who, with another member of the family, erected a marker on the spot. It is a massive granite boulder with a bronze plate bearing a replica of a pioneer cabin and the following inscription: "This stone marks the site of the log cabin home of 'Dicky Hanks', an uncle of Nancy Hanks, mother of Abraham Lincoln. Nancy spent much of her girlhood here with her uncle." The foundation stones on which the boulder was placed were once part of the chimney of the original cabin. Now a beautiful forest surrounds the place. At the foot of the hill, under spreading beeches, still bubbles the family spring where Nancy often quenched her thirst.

C. T. Stowe knew well the story of Nancy Hanks's residence here. He learned it from near neighbors of the Hankses with whom he was familiar and who knew both "Dicky" and Nancy well. One of them was Matthew Leeper, a Revolutionary soldier, who lived near the future site of the Hanks's home from the time of his birth in 1755 until his death in 1849, long after the Hankses had come and gone. Hugh Ewing, another Revolutionary soldier, lived close by. He was listed in the same census as "Dicky Hanks," and Samuel Ewing, a son of Hugh of Revolutionary fame, lived barely a stone's throw away. After the close of the War between the States, C. T. Stowe lived in the Samuel Ewing home with him until Mr. Ewing's death in 1872 and continued his residence there until 1880 when he moved into a new home.

Mr. Ewing was well acquainted with the Hankses, having signed the marriage bond of Richard II.

After the Hankses left the place, Mr. Ewing bought it and moved the logs of the Hanks's cabin to his own home where they were built into a granary. The same logs were again moved by C. T. Stowe, who had come into possession of the land for his new home, and built into a house for storing cotton. Again they were moved to another site on the C. T. Stowe farm where the cabin stands today, a reminder of a bit of interesting history connecting Nancy Hanks, the mother of Abraham Lincoln, with the annals of Gaston County.

CHAPTER XIV

In 1846 Gaston County was born of distinguished ancestry. It was erected from Lincoln in 1846, Lincoln from Tryon in 1779, Tryon from Mecklenburg in 1768 (effective April 4, 1769), Mecklenburg from Anson in 1762, Anson from Bladen in 1749, Bladen from New Hanover in 1734, New Hanover in 1729 from territory which had been Clarendon but was now Bath, Bath in 1696 from Albemarle, which for a time constituted the province of North Carolina. (Wager's County Government in North Carolina.)

The county was named for Judge William Gaston, Associate Justice of the Supreme Court of North Carolina. A brief sketch of his life will follow.

The record of the passage of the bill creating the county was taken from the Senate and House Journals of the General Assembly, 1846-47. From the House Journal we have the following: "The bill establishing the county was introduced in the House of Commons, November 20, 1846, by Gustavus A. Miller of Davie County. On November 24, Maurice Q. Waddell of Chatham County called the bill up for consideration. After discussion, the bill was referred to a select committee composed of Waddell, Daniel W. Courts of Rockingham County, John A. Fagg of Buncombe County, and Samuel

Flemming of Yancey County. On November 28, Waddell, of the committee, reported the bill out of committee with amendments. One of the amendments was to change the name from Gaston to Carroll, but it was voted down. The other amendments were voted in the affirmative. Then James H. White of Lincoln County made the motion to lay the bill on the table, which was carried. On December 2, James H. White called the bill from the table and offered amendments relative to the proposed boundary line, but the amendments did not carry and the bill passed the second reading, whereupon the rules were suspended and the bill passed the third reading and was ordered to be engrossed."

The following is from the Senate Journal: "On December 2, 1846, William Albright of Chatham, chairman of the committee on propositions and grievances, reported the bill to erect Gaston County with amendments. The bill was ordered to be tabled. On December 4, the Senate received a message from the House which said that it had ordered the bill to be engrossed and requested the Senate to concur in its passage. On December 5, Larkin Stowe of Lincoln and Catawba made a motion to take up the bill which was read the first time and passed; the rules were suspended and it was read the second time and passed, and on the motion of Mr. Stowe, it was read the third time and passed."

Samuel F. Patterson representing Burke, Caldwell, Wilkes, and McDowell Counties moved to reconsider the vote. This was not agreed to. On

December 18, John M. Bogle of Iredell moved to change the name to Alexander and offered other amendments which did not carry. This last motion seems to have been on the supplemental act and not on the act to establish the county.

As seen, the act was ratified December 5, 1846, and Isaac Holland, Andrew Love, and Jacob Plonk for Gaston, and John Coulter and Alexander Lowe for Lincoln, were named to survey the new and old counties.

The act also provided that commissioners be appointed to select a county site and call it Dallas for George Mifflin Dallas, Vice President of the United States under President Polk in 1844. The site was to be near the center of the county, not more than two miles from Long Creek Baptist Church.

The first County Court was held at the home of Jesse Holland on the 3rd Monday of February, 1847. The mistress of that home was Martha Hanks Holland, a daughter of "Dicky Hanks," the uncle of Nancy Hanks with whom Nancy made her home while he lived on the Catawba before he moved to the vicinity of Dallas.

It was through the generosity of Jesse Holland that the county came into possession of the court house property. From the seventy-five acres of land donated by him the courthouse square was set apart and the remainder sold off for building lots. The proceeds were applied to a building fund for the courthouse and jail.

That same year, 1847, a temporary courthouse of logs was built. It was ready for use by fall, 1847. A brick building was constructed in 1848. Twenty years later it was destroyed by fire, all but the walls and foundation. Most of the records, including court minutes and marriage bonds, were burned. However, some of the records were saved by the thoughtfulness of the women of Dallas who picked them up in their aprons. Among the items saved were the Wills and Deeds books.

The walls and foundation of the old building were used in the construction of the quaint, attractive building still standing on the courthouse square in Dallas. It is still loved and is full of interest to the people of the county, for there it was that their government functioned for many years.

On August 4, 1909, an election was held which resulted in the moving of the county seat to Gastonia and the building of a new courthouse there. The contents of the old courthouse were moved to this building January 1, 1911.

The old courthouse now belongs to the town of Dallas and is used as a school and community center, guarded and cherished by all that is best in the life of the town.

JUDGE WILLIAM GASTON

Judge William Gaston, for whom Gaston County was named, was born at New Bern, September 19, 1778. He was the son of Dr. Alexander Gaston, of French-Huguenot stock, and Margaret Sharpe Gaston, an English lady of Roman Catholic faith, who came to New Bern to visit her two brothers. Here she met Alexander Gaston and married him.

When Judge Gaston was three years old, his father was murdered before his and his mother's eyes by a band of Tories who invaded New Bern.

His early educational training was received at home under the supervision of his mother. He afterwards went to Georgetown College, later Georgetown University, which school he left because of ill health. Later he attended New Bern Academy and Princeton, where he graduated with first honors in 1796. After returning home he studied law under Francis Xavier Martin, a noted lawyer and historian.

His political career began in 1800. He served several terms in the State Legislature in the House and Senate and two terms in the U. S. Congress. He practiced his profession from the time he left Congress until 1833 when he was elected to fill a vacancy in the Supreme Court of North Carolina caused by the death of Judge Henderson.

Judge Gaston, in addition to his many other accomplishments, was both musician and poet. He wrote the words of North Carolina's State song, "The Old North State."

So far as is known, Judge Gaston was never in Gaston County, but had many interests here. When the little church of St. Joseph's was started in 1843, he was a liberal contributor. He stood before the whole country as a loyal Catholic whose influence was national.

Judge Gaston died in Raleigh, January 7, 1844, near the time of completion of St. Joseph's Church in the county which bears his name.

At a meeting of the Bar held in the courthouse at Lincolnton, March 17, 1844, resolutions were passed paying a glowing tribute to Judge Gaston, showing the esteem in which he was held as scholar, statesman, jurist, and Christian.

The old Gaston County Courthouse in Dallas, North Carolina. The current county courthouse is in Gastonia. (Photo courtesy of the Gaston County Museum of Art and History.)

CHAPTER XV

THE BEGINNING OF THE TEXTILE INDUSTRY
IN GASTON COUNTY

WOODLAWN MILL

The great textile industry of Gaston County, which began about the time the county was formed, was centered in three mills, two on the South Fork and one on the Catawba River. According to the best information obtainable, the Woodlawn was the first. The building was started in 1845 and began operation about the same time as the Stowe in 1848. It was located on the South Fork River one and one-half miles from Lowell.

The promoters were Caleb J. Lineberger, father of A. C. Lineberger, prominent textile man of Belmont, Caleb's brother, Laban, Lewis Lineberger, Moses H. Rhyne, John Clemmer, and Jonas Hoffman. Clemmer and Hoffman soon withdrew.

In the building of the mill, as far as possible, native materials were used. The foundation was of stone, the upper part wood. Because of primitive conditions the progress of the work was slow. Part of the machinery was purchased in Philadelphia, and the remainder came from England. All was landed at Charleston. From there it was sent by steam railroad to Branchville, S. C., and hauled from that place to the mill site on company wagons.

The mill was originally called Woodlawn, but at an early date acquired the name Pinhook by which it became almost universally known.

Because of its location on the road between Stowe's Factory and Mountain Island, it became an important trading center.

Contrary to now prevalent custom, the work of running the mill was divided among the owners as suited each one's ability. Laban Lineberger did the selling. The products of the mill were sometimes exchanged for country produce which was sold at the store run in connection with the mill. Three-fourth yard sheetings were made, and during the War between the States shirting for the soldiers. It was sold to merchants in North and South Carolina and delivered to them from four and six horse teams.

At first the business prospered and a large fortune was made which was mostly lost during the war. If bills were collected at all, payment was made in Confederate money which was without value. After the war 1,000 bales of cotton, worth in Europe $1.00 per pound in gold, were struck by lightning and destroyed. There was no insurance.

Finally the interests of the others were bought up by Caleb Lineberger. Part of the property is still in the hands of a son, A. C. Lineberger, of Belmont.

Could the murmuring river speak as it flows by the deserted ruins of the mill, it would tell of enterprise, achievement, and success followed by cruel disappointments in the wake of war.

Woodlawn Factory (Photo courtesy of the Gaston County Museum of Art and History.)

Mountain Island Mill (Photo courtesy of the Gaston County Museum of Art and History.)

A mill interior circa 1924. (Photo courtesy of the Gaston County Museum of Art and History.)

STOWE'S FACTORY AND COLONEL JASPER STOWE

Stowe's Factory and the name of Jasper Stowe are inseparably linked. The mill was finished in 1848, two years after Gaston was set up as a county. The Woodlawn Mill, or Pinhook as it was nicknamed, was started a little earlier than Stowe's, in 1845, but both began operations about the same time.

Stowe's was located on the South Fork River in the Point section of the county. Jasper Stowe was the force behind it. In connection with the mill there were a store and a large farm of eleven hundred acres lying on both sides of the river. Edwin Stowe, a brother of Jasper, had charge of the store and farm while Jasper ran the mill. The firm name was J. and E. B. Stowe. Yarns and plain unbleached cloth were manufactured.

In the early years of its operation most of the products were sold from wagons throughout the community. The yarns were used by the women for knitting, weaving, and other purposes. However, occasional shipments were hauled to Charleston until Woodlawn, now Mt. Holly, became the shipping point after the old Lincoln Railroad was built. Old "Uncle Tom," a family slave noted for two things, his devotion to the family and his big feet, was the wagoner. He would take the yarns and cloth to Woodlawn, cracking his whip over two big mules, and bring back the mail. The factory was then a post office known as Stowesville.

The late Dick Wooten, a Belmont man, whose early life was spent at Stowe's Factory, had in his possession a clock used in the mill when it was first built.

Jasper Stowe was a son of Larkin and Susan Spratt Neal Stowe and a grandson of Jacob and Nancy Ford Stowe. Jacob and his brother, Abraham, were the two pioneers of that name who came to this section from Virginia in 1810.

He was born February 27, 1821, at the Larkin Stowe home, more recently known as the Pegram place, in the New Hope neighborhood of the county. There he lived until he married Mrs. Julia Lecraft Parks of Beaufort, where they made their home for a time. They afterwards lived at the factory, moving from there to Lincolnton where they lived until the wife died. His brother, Edwin, also lost his wife about the same time. Both moved with their children to the factory where a sister, Miss Laura Stowe, later Mrs. H. D. Stowe of Steele Creek, carefully reared the children of both.

Jasper Stowe was a plain unassuming man, free from vanity, full of simplicity, and eager to be of service. Governor Vance said to him during the war: "Stowe, you shall not go to the army. No man in the South can take your place where you are." And it is true no man of the South did more for the women and children than he. They were furnished meat and corn from the farm and yarns from the mill. If a sale were made and payment received at all, it was in Confederate money which was of no value.

The close of the war found him in much reduced circumstances from which he never rallied. But his courage, kindness, and good cheer never failed him. His superior intellect remained undimmed until he was called by death, May 22, 1902, at the home of a brother, Colonel William A. Stowe near Belmont, by whom he lies buried in New Hope Cemetery.

MOUNTAIN ISLAND MILL

The Mountain Island Mill building was started in 1846 by Thomas Tate of Greensboro. The site was chosen for two reasons: one was that there was a partially constructed canal, originally intended to convey cotton to Charleston but which could be easily used for a race; the other was that water power was cheaper than steam. The name was chosen from the little mountain, now almost covered by water, and from Mt. Hechler Mill at Greensboro from which the machinery was moved and started up in its new home during the fall of 1849.

Mr. Tate was a son-in-law of Henry Humphrey who erected and operated the Mt. Hechler Mill at Greensboro. It was largely through marriage with Mr. Humphrey's daughter that Tate came into possession of it.

Short hours were unknown. In those days the mill was operated from sunup to sundown. Men's wages were from twenty-five to forty cents a day. Women received the same for weaving. The pay of small boys was from five to twenty-five cents. There was no age limit and free schools were unknown;

consequently, there was nothing else for the children to do but to work.

Heavy sheeting was manufactured. Nos. 8, 10, and 12 yarns, put up in 5-pound bunches and wrapped in blue paper, were sold mostly over North Carolina and Tennessee. The sheeting was left plain for underclothing and men's shirts. For women's dresses and other uses it was dyed with copperas or maple bark. Sumac berries were sometimes used in the colors.

There was a wool department during the war; blankets and Southern gray for the soldiers were made by Negro slave labor. There was no longer anything with which to pay white help. Barter had formerly been used.

The plant closed down at the surrender and remained closed until 1872. In 1884 the Tates sold the mill to William J. Hopper of Baltimore.

Some of the Tate family had moved away; others had died. Many changes took place until finally during the great flood of 1916 the entire plant was washed away.

Mr. George Tate, of McAdenville, is a grandson of Thomas Tate, founder of the Mountain Island Mill, and is one of the few members of the family left in the county.

CHAPTER XVI

CATHOLICISM IN GASTON COUNTY

ST. JOSEPH'S CHURCH

About two miles from Mt. Holly on the Mountain Island road is the quaint little Catholic church, at first called Sts. Mary and Joseph, though now simply named St. Joseph.

It was in the Diocese of Charleston, founded in 1820 by Bishop England and comprised of the two Carolinas and Georgia.

All eastern North Carolina was a mission of that diocese with small stations at several points. The first Catholic church in the state was built at New Bern about 1830 by the family of Judge William Gaston, the second at Fayetteville, and the third at Raleigh. St. Joseph's was the fourth.

In the western part of the state there were also many small and scattered missions occasionally visited by clergymen of the diocese.

In the days before St. Joseph's was built, mines were opened in the vicinity by Chevalier Riva De Finola, a devout Catholic, who worked them from 1828-1835. During that period scattered families of Irish Catholics, including the Lonegans, Cahills, Duffys, Coxes, Millers, Hawkinses, and others, settled in the community, attracted probably by the mining interests or the Chevalier's hospitable home where a welcome always awaited and where a chapel was provided for visiting clergy, especially Bishop England.

For some time the early Catholic settlers had no church, but eventually a few acres of land for church purposes were donated by William Lonegan to Father Cronin, who had been sent from Charleston to take charge of the missions in the western part of the state. His zeal and self-sacrifice deserve commendation by all.

Father Cronin was born and reared in Cork, Ireland, but was educated for the priesthood in Charleston. He was weakened by yellow fever when he was assigned the Western North Carolina district.

His work was hard; physically he was impaired. He had no home, no church. For four years he lived from house to house, not knowing where he would spend the night or get the next meal. He preached when he could find a suitable place.

Lands for a church had been secured, but before sufficient funds could be raised for its erection Father Cronin died, in the autumn of 1842, at Salisbury. He was first buried there, but his remains were later transferred to Gaston County to the land that had been donated to him for a church and burying ground. The lonely isolation of the grave strongly appealed to Catholics over the diocese, and generous contributions poured in from so many sources that Father John Guifford, the succeeding priest, saw St. Joseph's built on the land donated by William Lonegan.

The building was begun in 1843. It was completed, free from debt, and dedicated within two

Belmont Abbey

The College Building at Belmont Abbey was built in three stages during the late 1800s. This portico, at the main entrance, was designed by the prominent ecclesiastical architect Dom Michael McInerney, O.S.B., a monk of the abbey, and erected in 1902. The building was renamed Robert Lee Stowe Hall in 1983. *(Photo courtesy of the Archives of Belmont Abbey.)*

Built in 1843, the Church of Saint Mary and Saint Joseph was the fourth Catholic church in the state. St. Joseph Church, as it is more widely known, is still standing, north of Mount Holly in Gaston County. *(Photo courtesy of the Archives of Belmont Abbey.)*

The Abbey Cathedral of Maryhelp at Belmont Abbey was the largest Catholic church in North Carolina at the time of its construction (1892-1893). Pictured here is the Mass in 1910 whereat Belmont Abbey was raised to diocesan rank. This was to be the only monastery in the country ever to win that designation. *(Photo courtesy of the Archives of Belmont Abbey.)*

The Sisters of Mercy came to Gaston County in 1892. They soon developed a prosperous religious foundation, with schools, hospitals, an orphanage, and other ministries. Renowned Catholics often visited Sacred Heart and Belmont campuses. Pictured here are students assembled for one such occasion in the early days of Sacred Heart. *(Photo courtesy of the Archives of Belmont Abbey.)*

St. Benedict Church was built ca. 1886 by Bishop Leo Haid, O.S.B., the first abbot of Belmont. Located on property north of the college, the church was converted to an elementary school in 1894. The gathering of students and families featured here took place in the late 1910s or early 1920s. The priest is Father Gerard Rettger. *(Photo courtesy of the Archives of Belmont Abbey.)*

years. The Hon. William Gaston, for whom Gaston County was named, was a liberal contributor.

In 1847 when Father Guifford left the mission, he had succeeded in making St. Joseph's a firmly fixed religious center. For several years there were no regularly established priests, but there were supplies. One of these, Dr. J. J. O'Connell, wrote a delightful history of "Catholicity in the Carolinas and Georgia," published in 1878. It has kept alive the early records of St. Joseph and its loyal members who lie buried within the stone wall enclosure surrounding the church and cemetery.

St. Joseph's remained a part of the Diocese of Charleston until 1869 when North Carolina was created a separate vicariate by Pope Pius IX. The Right Reverend James Gibbons, D.D., who was later Cardinal, was made the first vicar apostolic.

As Bishop of North Carolina, he found St. Joseph's a well-established church which he visited several times for confirmations and communion services. Miss Mary Smith of Stanley and her sister, Mrs. Kate Leeper of Belmont, were confirmed by the great prelate.

Dr. O'Connell had lived and worked for many years in Columbia, S. C., but after the close of the War between the States his duties often brought him to western North Carolina.

During the fall of 1872, Dr. O'Connell purchased the Caldwell place, a settlement dating back to Colonial times. After the purchase he restored it to order and then deeded it to the Right Reverend James Gibbons for the building of a religious and educational male institution. Dr. Gibbons immediately negotiated with the Benedictines of St. Vincent's of Westmoreland County, Pa. The donation consisted of everything on the premises.

In the spring of 1876, Rev. Herman Wolfe, O.S.B., arrived and after a thorough examination accepted the gift. He returned to St. Vincent's, and all that he had done was approved by the Chapter and sanctioned by the venerable Abbot Wimmer. Father Wolfe with four brothers came back, took possession, and entered on their duties.

Little was accomplished the first year. In June, 1877, the Abbot visited the institution, called it St. Mary of Help, directed the building of a commodious chapel, and furnished an organ. He also gave instructions to erect a college building. Thus began the first Catholic college in the middle South for the education of boys.

In 1884 Archabbot Wimmer determined to make the Southern Benedictine Mission independent. The arrangement was confirmed by a Papal Brief and the community of Belmont received the official title, Maryhelp Abbey. From St. Vincent's four priests and six clerics volunteered to go to North Carolina. On July 14, Father Leo Haid, O.S.B., an able professor and assistant rector of St. Vincent's College, was elected Abbot of the new Abbey. In 1886 the College received its charter from the state, and the cornerstone was laid for the erection of a new college building. On St. Benedict's day, March 21, 1892, ground was broken for the new Abbey Church. It was dedicated in 1894 by Cardinal Gib-

bons in the presence of a large concourse of distinguished guests. The building is a magnificent speci-
men of Gothic architecture with a beautifully deco-
rated interior. The stained glass windows are said
to be the finest in America, having received the first
prize at the Chicago World's Fair in 1893.

In 1887 Pope Leo XIII appointed Father Leo
Haid as Vicar Apostolic and Titular Bishop of
North Carolina. The name of Maryhelp Abbey was
changed in 1913 to Belmont Abbey by which it is
still known. Under the wise leadership of Bishop
Haid the Fathers of Belmont carried the work into
three other Southern states, Georgia, Florida, and
Virginia, without curtailing, in the least, their
activities in North Carolina. Bishop Leo Haid died
June 24, 1924, after a long and arduous life during
which he had seen his work grow and prosper. He
was succeeded by the Right Reverend Vincent
George Taylor, O.S.B., who is the present Ordinary
of Belmont Abbey.

SISTERS OF MERCY

The history of the Sisters of Mercy, who established The Sacred Heart Academy and have had an
integral part in the development of Catholicism in
Gaston County, dates back nearly three-quarters of
a century. In several places there were communities
of these Sisters before the permanent Motherhouse
was erected in Belmont.

Their work was at first punctuated by manifold
hardships and impending threats of failure, but with
two fundamentals, education and charity, they

pressed forward until their efforts were crowned with success.

After they had established a school in Charlotte in 1887, Bishop Haid requested that they begin educational work in Belmont, which they agreed to do.

A letter from Bishop Haid dated October 18, 1891, conveyed the news to the Sisters that he had been offered a piece of property between the monastery and the town of Belmont. The purchase of the land was made and the Sisters moved to Belmont on September 1, 1892. The Sacred Heart Academy opened the same month with twenty-one students.

In September, 1894, St. Ann's Orphanage for girls was opened at the Motherhouse.

For about twenty years the Sisters conducted St. Benedict's School for colored children. Now a paid worker teaches the children until they reach the seventh grade when they go to Reid High School.

Under the wise, efficient leadership of Mother M. Teresa, who guided the institution in its early days and who is still remembered as a most unusual woman and business executive, the work of the Sisters of Mercy got a good start and is still prospering.

It is a significant fact that the great Cardinal who used to visit the little church of St. Joseph wrought its fate by establishing not far from it the fine Belmont Abbey Cathedral. Since the opening of the Cathedral most of the members of St. Joseph's have left and joined there. Many of the old families of the Gaston County Mission have moved near the school and Cathedral.

CHAPTER XVII

THE WAR BETWEEN THE STATES

Many years had passed since Major Chronicle led the "South Fork boys" up the slope of King's Mountain when again the men of Gaston County buckled on their swords, took up their trusty rifles, and went forth to engage in the fratricidal strife of the War between the States. For four long years the bloody strife went on before the flag of the Confederacy was furled and the hopes of the South drooped and died.

The first of the soldiers to go out from Gaston County were volunteers who enlisted at Brevard Station, now Stanley, May 1, 1861. They were known as Company M, 6th N. C. Regular Volunteers, with B. F. Briggs, Captain.

Many people went to Brevard Station to see the soldiers off. That town was at the time the terminal of the Seaboard Airline Railroad and during the war was the tithing station of Gaston County for the Confederacy.

The soldiers went to Raleigh where on June 17, 1861, with other N. C. Volunteers, Company M of Gaston County became part of the 16th N. C. Regiment with Stephen Lee of Buncombe County as Colonel. The twelve companies were made up of those of the state who were first to volunteer. Many were from the mountains and all were in the bloom of young manhood, most of them unmarried. After the organization and before future campaigns had wrought devastating effects, it is said that the citizens of Raleigh and Richmond remarked upon the fulness of the regiment and its faultless personnel.

After leaving Raleigh, the regiment arrived in Richmond on July 6, 1861. It was at Valley Mountain that the 16th Regiment first got a glimpse of General Lee. They saw in him a man, a leader who from the beginning inspired their courage and kept it up until the end. The 16th Regiment was at first attached to Hampton's Legion and went to Yorktown where it was reorganized on April 26, 1862. William Stowe of Gaston County was elected major. He had enlisted as a private in the regular N. C. Volunteers at Brevard Station, May 1, 1861. The next day after the regiment was organized, on June 18, 1861, he was made a captain. The list of his promotions until he was a full colonel are given in the sketch of his life which will follow later. Colonel Stowe was the highest ranking officer who went out from Gaston County.

At the battle of Seven Pines which began May 21, 1862, the 16th Regiment lost some of its ablest officers and men. Benjamin Cathey in Clark's "North Carolina Regiments" says: "The enemy used in front of the 16th Regiment some large New-foundland dogs as advance pickets. When our picket line moved forward these quadruped Yankees were disposed of in short order by leaden pellets."

The 16th Regiment saw much hard fighting. It participated in the battles of Seven Pines, Cedar Run, Sharpsburg, Mechanicsville, Manassas, Shepherdstown, Gaine's Mill, Ox Hill, Fredericksburg, Frazier's Farm, Harper's Ferry, Gettysburg, and many others. The names of battles were embroidered on its flag until it was full. Others were embroidered on ribbons and tied to the staff.

After the first volunteers there were six companies that went out from Gaston County. In the lists of material compiled by the late L. M. Hoffman of Dallas, he gives the roll of the original members and also of the officers with rank and whether commissioned or non-commissioned. Sometimes there were more, but usually ten companies made a regiment. Since Gaston did not have enough men in the early days of the war for a regiment, the six full companies helped to make up Regiments 16, 23, 28, 37, 49, and 71. As the war went on, the ranks of all the regiments were so depleted by capture, wounds, illness, and death that other men enlisting from the county were placed where needed. So there were many who joined companies not formed in the county. Therefore, Gaston does not get credit for the number of men actually furnished.

The going of the men and the subsequent deaths filled the county with gloom, but a sadder day was yet to come when the Junior Reserves, mere children, marched away to battle for the Confederacy.

There were not enough seventeen-year-old boys to form a company, so the Lincoln County boys were added to those of Gaston and formed Company C of the 2nd Regiment, N. C. Junior Reserves. They later became a part of the 71st Regiment.

Company C was made up altogether of boys between seventeen and eighteen. Ninety-five of them were from Gaston, seventy-one from Lincoln, and one from North Hampton. The one from North Hampton was named Beal, a retired regular who was made an officer in the new company.

The company was organized May 24, 1864, and met in Charlotte where the boys slept in the depot at night on bags of grain. Temporary officers were elected before going to Raleigh where they camped and drilled for several weeks. The Lincoln County boys joined them there. The entire number was now 167. A permanent organization was effected and Mr. J. Q. Holland was made captain. Most of the officers were from Gaston. The Juniors participated in the small battles of Hicksford, or Belfield, Va., Kinston, and Bentonsville, N. C., and surrendered at or near High Point. A short time before they laid down their arms, Mr. G. W. Ragan was chosen color bearer and the flag was turned over to him by Captain Holland.

THE FLAG OF THE 16TH N. C. REGIMENT

In the Hall of History, Raleigh, there are two flags of especial interest to this section—the colors of the 16th N. C. Regiment, Colonel William A. Stowe commanding. Company M of the 16th Regiment was composed largely of Gaston County men. Each regiment was entitled to two flags. One was a Confederate battle flag which was borne into battle. On the battle flag was the name of the state and the number of the regiment. The second, or state flag, did not figure prominently on the battlefield. In the official book of Confederate Army Regulations there seems to be no rule concerning its use. The battle flag of the 16th Regiment was captured at Gettysburg, July 3, 1863, by the 14th Connecticut Volunteers. To replace the captured flag, another was made by Miss R. C. Semon of Richmond and presented to the 16th Regiment.

In 1905 the Hall of History was established during the term of office of Governor Glenn, who was instrumental, through W. H. Taft, then Secretary of War, and President Theodore Roosevelt, in having all flags carried by N. C. troops and captured by Northern soldiers returned to the State. That same year the flag of the 16th Regiment, captured at Gettysburg, was returned by Connecticut and entrusted to the late Colonel Fred Olds, then and for years afterwards curator of the Hall of History.

The flag made by Miss Semon and presented to the 16th Regiment is the one that connects two Gaston County soldier boys, Emanuel Rudisill of the Beaver Dam section of Cherryville Township and James Pinckney Stowe of the Belmont section.

Emanuel Rudisill, incited perhaps by the fact that he had nine brothers in the army, enlisted March 17, 1862, and joined Company M of the 16th Regiment.

On August 22, 1863, James Pinckney Stowe, then a boy of eighteen, volunteered and also joined Company M, 16th N. C. Regiment at Orange Court House, Va. Rudisill and Stowe became fast friends and stuck closely together until the end of the war.

Stowe was a sharpshooter and was in many a vanguard skirmish. Near the close of the war the color bearer, whose name was not known, was shot down. Stowe picked up the flag and guarded it until another color bearer could be appointed. Young Rudisill was selected and served until the end of the war. In Vol. 5, p. 552, Clarke's "North Carolina Regiments," there is a list of the officers of the 16th Regiment paroled at Appomattox. Emanuel Rudisill's name appears in the list as color sergeant. However, he was not present at the surrender. With his friend Stowe and two other boys, Wiley McKee and John Jarrett, he stopped to cook something to eat and was cut off from the regiment which went on to Appomattox and surrendered.

Learning that the surrender had already taken place, the boys decided to go on home. But what should they do with the flag? They knew it must be preserved, so Stowe and Rudisill ripped it from its staff, sewed it in the lining of Rudisill's coat, and brought it home. It was never surrendered; nor did the boys surrender, but after the war they took the oath of allegiance to the government of the reunited states. With Colonel William Stowe's permission, the flag remained in Rudisill's possession. A sister cared for it and carried it to him in Texas after he had moved there.

In 1919, when Bickett was Governor, this flag was also turned over to the Hall of History where the two, battle-scarred as they are, rest in their cases, the pride of Gaston County and the State.

COLONEL WILLIAM A. STOWE

Colonel Stowe, or "Colonel Bill" as he was called, was born in the New Hope section of the county, January 31, 1832, of English stock. He was the son of Larkin and Susan Spratt Neal Stowe and grandson of Jacob Stowe who came to North Carolina from Virginia in 1810. His early life, with the exception of a short period in York, South Carolina, was spent on his father's plantation where he was born.

He never married but held a high place in the esteem and friendship of his neighbors, among whom he visited often. Big-hearted, generous, and kind, he appealed especially to little children who loved him dearly. For them he always had a pleasant word and usually a pocketful of candy or something for their pleasure. His early life was that of a handsome, courtly country gentleman whom the slaves on his father's plantation delighted to honor as "Marse Bill."

When the echoes of war began resounding, "Colonel Bill," with many of his neighbors and friends, offered his services to the state. He enlisted as a private, May 1, 1861, in Company M, 6th N. C. Regular Volunteers. The next day after the regiment was organized in Raleigh on June 17, 1861, he was made captain.

The regiment, after its organization, remained in Raleigh drilling and performing guard duty until July 5, when it left for the seat of war. The next year, on April 26, 1862, it was reorganized at Yorktown and William A. Stowe was elected major. On May 31, 1862, he was made lieutenant colonel. At Chancellorsville Colonel John S. McElroy was severely wounded. Lieutenant Colonel Stowe assumed command and on December 8, 1863, he was commissioned a full colonel, which position he occupied until the end of the war.

The flag of the 16th Regiment was carried into many battles, and numbers of the men gave up their lives before the conquered banner was finally furled. Colonel Stowe did not spare himself. He was twice wounded, once severely in the defense of Richmond. A bullet penetrated his skull and lodged in the back of his neck. It was never extracted. Those carrying the wounded from the field noticed his uniform and said, "He is a colonel; we will take him, though he will be dead before we reach help." He didn't die but lived to a ripe old age, never ceasing to regret that he had to carry "Yankee lead" around with him, which he did to the day of his death.

Colonel Stowe was a gallant and successful commander. His record was one of the best. Wiley McKee, one of his soldiers, said of him: " 'Colonel Bill' was one of the most popular soldiers of the Southern army, always considerate of his men. When it was necessary to punish, it was done in the most humane way."

After Petersburg the 16th Regiment, still un-daunted, dividing the corn of the horses to appease hunger and stubbornly marching and fighting to the last, surrendered with Lee at Appomattox. Their sacrifices were fully repaid when, the dread day having arrived and the momentous act per-formed, they listened to the following words as they fell from the lips of General Lee himself, "God bless old North Carolina."

COLONEL WILLIAM MORRIS

William Groves Morris was born on Dutchman's Creek in Gaston County on November 20, 1825. Near the outbreak of the War between the States he enlisted for service and became the second highest ranking officer who went out from Gaston County. He joined Company H of the 37th Regiment. He was promoted from major to lieutenant colonel and commissioned on May 29, 1863.

Colonel Morris was in many battles and saw much hard fighting and was twice wounded.

On the retreat from Sharpsburg the Confederate army was sorely pressed when General A. P. Hill ordered Major Morris, then in command of the rear guards, to about-face and charge the enemy. One color bearer after another was shot down. Major Morris seized the colors and rushed with them into the thick of the battle.

Once when the 37th Regiment was receiving a baptism of fire and threw itself flat on the edge of the turnpike, Morris remained standing although his friends urged him to lie down. This he refused to do. Soon a piece of shell struck him in the foot. "See there," he exclaimed, "if I had been lying down it would have struck me in the head."

At Chancellorsville, though wounded, he assisted in reforming the 37th Regiment. At Gettysburg he was captured with twenty of his comrades after crossing the enemy's breastworks. Not wanting the "Yankees" to get his sword he broke it between the logs of a near-by barn.

After the capture he was imprisoned at Johnston's Island for eighteen months.

When he returned home, he engaged in farming and served one term in the Legislature from 1876-1877. Colonel Morris died at his old home near Dallas in 1918, at the ripe old age of 93.

Their sacrifices [the 16th Regiment] were fully repaid when, the dread day having arrived... they listened to the following words as they fell from the lips of General Lee himself, "God bless old North Carolina."

CHAPTER XVIII

LATER HAPPENINGS IN THE COUNTY

Gaston County is worthy of a volume that would take up the story and chronicle the interesting incidents of all the soldiers who fought so nobly for the county and the Confederacy. The record would be one of bravery and courage, unparalleled in the annals of history.

The Southern soldier was overcome by overwhelming numbers and forced to lay down his arms.

The war was over but the new horror of the Reconstruction period gripped the South, but that, too, came to an end. The farmer settled down to his plowing again, the birds sang sweetly, the squirrels chattered in the trees, and the flowers bloomed in the vales and died untrampled by busy feet.

The wooded hills near the Catawba in the southern part of the county were unbroken. No railroad cuts severed them. After a while, a rumor was heard that a railroad was coming. It proved to be true. In 1870 work was in progress on the Gaston side of the river. By 1873 the road had reached Gastonia.

It was glad news for the people. They knew that now many closed doors would be open to them. Their forests would yield crossties and cord wood, for the trains were wood burners in those days;

stores would be opened, educational facilities improved, and rail traffic would be accessible for all. A new era would begin.

The hopes of the people were realized; they now had a market for farm supplies. It was easy to obtain what they needed not produced on the farms. Through the mails they kept in touch with the outside world. The log schoolhouses were replaced by those planked up and down or weatherboarded and ceiled.

Then with the beginning of the great textile industry the modern brick buildings which now dot the county began to be constructed.

They are the outcome of the development which has made Gaston County the center of the combed yarn industry of America. Cotton mills sprang up over the county until we now have more separate corporations than any county in the world.

While farming is still carried on extensively in some parts of the county, manufacturing has become the principal industry.

We were going forward as a happy, prosperous people, feeling so secure that we thought nothing could shake us from our position, but something did. One of the saddest episodes in the history of the county was yet to come. Our own boys, boys we had known from childhood, some of them from babyhood, were called to the camps, then sent to ports of embarkation and across the seas to engage in the great World War. Many of them now sleep under their crosses in foreign lands. They died for an ideal. They died that the world should have permanent peace. A hope which now, alas, seems so far away.

Gaston County, though young and small, has developed from what was little more than an American frontier when set up to a place second to none in the great galaxy of North Carolina counties, and has become one of the foremost and the best.

After a while, a rumor was heard that a railroad was coming. It proved to be true. . . . A new era would begin.

Stowe Mercantile Company *(Photo courtesy of the Gaston County Museum of Art and History.)*

The William Rankin home (Photo courtesy of the Gaston County Museum of Art and History.)

The house of Dr. John D. McLean, prior to renovation by Daniel J. Stowe *(Photo courtesy of the Gaston County Museum of Art and History.)*

INDEX

Rock

Statesville

Livevsville

Bunkers H.

Poplar Gr.

Airyvle

Branchvill

McElla

Jacobs R.

Murray R.

Jacobs R.

Newton

Winthrew

CATAWBA

LINE

Box
Bee

Poor C.

Jacobs C.

Brittle Fort

Mountain Gr.

Lincolnton

Mountain Gr.

LINCOLN

Catawba Spr.

Tho Horn

Caddle

Toward Cr.

Indian C.

Cottage

Home

River

Hukewell

Marti

Woylesville

Mountan

Howle

Hog

Woodlawn

Charlotte

Muddy C.

Dallas

Crowders

Catawba

White Hall

Sprangs I.

GASTON

Plains

McAlpin

Prov

As Mountn

Crowders Cr.

Crow

Bethany

Bethel

Stowesville

Pleasant

eeks Hill

Fort Mills

YORK

Yorkville

Bullocks Hill

Philadelphia

Ebenezer V.

Blairs V.

Clawetons Store

McConnells

Wax

Belle